ARSÈNE LUPIN
GENTLEMAN BURGLAR

MAURICE LEBLANC

TRANSLATED BY
LIAM FEROUSSE

Copyright © 2024 by Liam Ferousse

All rights reserved.

This book has been translated from the original French text, which is in the public domain. No part of this book may be reproduced in any form or by any electronic or mechanical means, including information storage and retrieval systems, without written permission from the author, except for the use of brief quotations in a book review.

ISBN: 9798345302590

To Pierre LAFITTE.

My dear friend,

You have led me down a path that I never thought I would venture, and I have found so much pleasure and literary enjoyment that it seems right to place your name at the beginning of this first volume and to express here my feelings of affectionate and loyal gratitude.

M. L.

INTRODUCTION

Arsène Lupin, Gentleman Burglar introduces readers to one of literature's most iconic anti-heroes, a master thief as charming as he is elusive. Created by Maurice Leblanc in 1907, Arsène Lupin is no ordinary criminal; he's a gentleman with a taste for the finer things, a code of honor, and a remarkable skill for outwitting society. In this collection, Lupin's escapades play out with wit and sophistication, as he delights in the art of the heist and the thrill of staying one step ahead of the law.

Each story reveals another layer of Lupin's complex character—a thief who targets the wealthy and corrupt, yet maintains his own unique sense of justice. From elaborate disguises to unexpected twists, Lupin's adventures span grand Parisian mansions to hidden retreats, where he navigates high society with grace, daring, and a mischievous charm. He enchants his targets, confounds the police, and, with flair and style, embodies a blend of humor, mystery, and sophistication that has captivated readers for generations.

With suspense, elegance, and humor, *Arsène Lupin, Gentleman Burglar* is a perfect introduction to Leblanc's gentleman thief. This edition brings the timeless appeal of Leblanc's tales to modern readers, offering a journey into a world of high-stakes heists, clever deception, and the thrill of the chase. Perfect for fans of mystery and classic adventure, Lupin remains the ultimate master of the art of the steal.

PREFACE

—So tell us, you who tell stories so well, a tale of thieves...

—Very well, said Voltaire (or another philosopher of the 18e century, as the anecdote is attributed to several of these incomparable conversationalists).

And he began:

—Once upon a time, there was a general farmer...

The author of the Adventures of Arsène Lupin, who also knows how to tell a story so charmingly, would have begun quite differently:

—Once upon a time, there was a gentleman thief...

And this paradoxical beginning would have raised the startled heads of the listeners. The adventures of Arsène Lupin, as incredible and captivating as those of Arthur Gordon Pym, have done even better. They did not just interest a select few; they captivated the masses. Since the day this astonishing character made his debut in Je sais tout, he has frightened, charmed, and entertained hundreds of thousands of readers, and in the new format of a book, he will triumphantly enter the library after conquering the magazine.

These stories of detectives and high-life or street criminals have always held a unique and powerful allure. Balzac, upon leaving Mme de Morsauf, lived the dramatic life of a police detective. He left behind the valley lily for the reluctant stream. Victor Hugo created Javert, chasing Jean Valjean just as the other "inspector" pursued Vautrin. And both were thinking of Vidocq, that strange wolf-catcher turned watchdog, from whom the poet of Les Misérables and the novelist of Rubempré had gathered confidences. Later, in a lesser order, Monsieur Lecoq sparked the curiosity of fans of detective fiction, and Mr. Bismarck and Mr. de Beust, these two adversaries—one fierce, the other witty—found, before and after Sadowa, what divided them the least: the tales of Gaboriau.

It often happens that a writer encounters a character on his path, creating a type that, in turn, brings literary fortune to its creator. Blessed is the one who invents an entirely new being that soon seems as alive as the living: Delobelle or Priola! The English novelist Conan Doyle popularized Sherlock Holmes. Mr. Maurice Leblanc found his own Sherlock Holmes, and I believe that since the exploits of the illustrious English detective, not a single adventure in the world has stirred curiosity as much as those of Arsène Lupin, a series of events that has now become a book.

The success of Mr. Leblanc's stories has been nothing short of explosive in the monthly magazine where readers, who once settled for the mundane plots of serialized novels, now seek (a significant evolution) literature that entertains them while still remaining literature.

The author began, if I'm not mistaken, about twelve years ago in the old Gil Blas, where his original short stories, sober and powerful, quickly placed him among the top storytellers. A native of Normandy, from Rouen, the author clearly belonged to the esteemed lineage of Flaubert, Maupassant, and Albert Sorel (who was also a short story writer in his time). His first novel, A Woman, garnered significant attention, and since then, several psychological studies such as The Work of Death, Armelle and Claude, Enthusiasm, a three-act play that was well-received at Antoine's, and Pity, have been added to the collection of his short novels of two hundred lines, where Mr. Maurice Leblanc excels.

One must have a particular gift for imagination to create such brief dramas, such quick stories that encapsulate the very essence of entire volumes, just as masterful vignettes contain fully formed paintings. These rare qualities of an inventive mind were bound to, at some point, find a broader scope, and the author of *Une Femme* was soon to focus after having scattered himself across so many original tales.

It was then that he encountered the delightful and unexpected Arsène Lupin.

The story of this 18th-century bandit is well known; he robbed people with elegance, much like Buffon wrote his *Histoire Naturelle*. Arsène Lupin is a great-nephew of this scoundrel who both terrified and charmed the frightened yet captivated marquises.

"You can compare," Mr. Marcel L'Heureux told me as he brought the proofs of his colleague's work and the issues where Je sais tout illustrated the exploits of Arsène Lupin, "you can compare Sherlock Holmes to Lupin and Maurice Leblanc to Conan Doyle. It's clear that the two writers have points of contact. Both possess the same narrative power, the same skill in plotting, the same understanding of mystery, the same rigorous connection of facts, and the same restraint in their methods. But there is a distinct superiority in the choice of subjects and in the very quality of the drama! And notice this feat: with Sherlock Holmes, we face a new theft and a new crime each time; here, we know in advance that Arsène Lupin is the culprit; we know that once we have unraveled the tangled threads of the story, we will find ourselves confronted with the famous gentleman thief! There was indeed a pitfall there. It has been avoided, and it would have been impossible to avoid it more skillfully than Maurice Leblanc has done. Using methods that even the most discerning cannot identify, he keeps you on the edge of your seat until the conclusion of each adventure. Until the very last line, we remain in uncertainty, curiosity, and anxiety, and the plot twist is always unexpected, shocking, and unsettling. Truly, Arsène Lupin is a character, a character already legendary, and one that will endure. A vibrant figure, young, full of cheer, unpredictability, and irony. A thief and burglar, a con artist and trickster—whatever you wish to call him, but how charming this bandit is! He acts with such delightful nonchalance! So much irony, so much charm, and so much wit! He is a dilettante. He is an artist! Mark this well: Arsène Lupin does not steal; he enjoys stealing. He chooses. If necessary, he returns it. He is noble and charming, chivalrous, delicate, and I repeat, so sympathetic that everything he does seems right, and one finds oneself unexpectedly hoping for the success of his endeavors, rejoicing in it, and even morality seems to be on his side. All of this, I repeat, because Lupin is the creation of an artist, and because in composing a book where he freely unleashed his imagination, Maurice Leblanc did not forget that he was, above all, and in every sense of the term, a writer!"

Thus spoke Mr. Marcel L'Heureux, a keen judge in the matter who knows the value of a novel, having written some truly remarkable ones himself. And I find myself in agreement with him after reading these ironically amusing pages, which are not at all immoral despite the paradox that so seduces the gentleman thief of his contemporaries. Certainly, I would not award a Montyon Prize to this very charming Lupin. But would we have crowned Fra Diavolo for his virtue, who captivated our grandmothers at the Opéra-Comique, in the distant time when the symbols of Ariadne and Bluebeard had not yet been invented?

Here he comes,

The red feather in his hat...

Arsène Lupin is a Fra Diavolo armed not with a blunderbuss, but with a revolver, dressed not in a romantic velvet coat, but in a properly tailored tuxedo, and I hope he enjoys the success that surpasses that of the irresistible bandit that Mr. Auber made famous in song.

But really! There is nothing to wish for Arsène Lupin. He has entered the realm of popularity alive. And the trend that the magazine has so well initiated will be continued by the book.

Jules CLARETIE.

CHAPTER ONE
THE ARREST OF ARSÈNE LUPIN

The strange journey! It had started off so well! For my part, I have never embarked on one that promised such happy auspices. The Provence is a swift, comfortable transatlantic liner, commanded by the most affable of men. The most select society was gathered aboard. Connections were forming, entertainments were being organized. We had that exquisite feeling of being separated from the world, reduced to ourselves as if on an unknown island, and thus obliged to draw closer to one another.

And we drew closer...

Have you ever thought about the originality and unpredictability of this gathering of beings who, just the day before, did not know each other, and who, for a few days, between the infinite sky and the vast sea, will live the most intimate life together, challenging the wrath of the Ocean, the terrifying assault of the waves, the malice of storms, and the treacherous calm of the still water?

It is, in essence, life itself experienced in a sort of tragic shortcut, with its storms and grandeur, its monotony and diversity, and perhaps that is why one savors this brief journey with a feverish haste and an even more intense pleasure, seeing its end even as it begins.

However, for several years now, something has been happening that adds significantly to the emotions of the crossing. The small floating island is still dependent on this world from which one thought they had escaped. A connection remains, which only gradually unravels in the open Ocean, and little by little, in the open Ocean, it is reestablished. The wireless telegraph! A call from another universe from which we would receive news in the most mysterious way possible! The imagination can no longer conjure up iron wires through which the invisible message glides. The mystery is even deeper, more poetic as well, and it is to the wings of the wind that we must turn to explain this new miracle.

Thus, in the first hours, we felt ourselves followed, escorted, even preceded by that distant voice, which now and then whispered to one of us a few words from afar. Two friends spoke to me. Ten others, twenty others, sent us all their saddened or smiling farewells across the space.

On the second day, five hundred miles off the French coast, during a stormy afternoon, the wireless telegraph sent us a message that read:

"Arsène Lupin on board, first class, blond hair, injury to the right forearm, traveling alone, under the name of R…"

At that precise moment, a loud clap of thunder erupted in the dark sky. The electric waves were interrupted. The rest of the message did not reach us. We only knew the initial of the name under which Arsène Lupin was hiding.

If it had been any other news, I have no doubt that the secret would have been scrupulously kept by the telegraph staff, as well as by the ship's commissioner and the captain. But there are certain events that seem to force the most stringent discretion. That very day, without anyone knowing how the information had leaked, we all knew that the famous Arsène Lupin was hiding among us.

Arsène Lupin among us! The elusive burglar whose exploits had been recounted in newspapers for months! The enigmatic figure with whom old Ganimard, our best policeman, had engaged in that deadly duel whose episodes unfolded in such a picturesque manner! Arsène Lupin, the whimsical gentleman who only operates in castles and salons, and who, one night, after breaking into Baron Schormann's home, left empty-handed and left his card, adorned with the phrase: "Arsène Lupin, gentleman burglar, will return when the furniture is authentic." Arsène Lupin, the man of a thousand disguises: at various times a chauffeur, tenor, bookmaker, son of a wealthy family, teenager, old man, traveling salesman from Marseille, Russian doctor, Spanish bullfighter!

Let's take a moment to consider this: Arsène Lupin, coming and going within the relatively confined space of a transatlantic ship—what am I saying!—in this small area of the first-class section where one could run into each other at any moment, in the dining room, in the lounge, in the smoking room! Arsène Lupin could have been that gentleman... or that one over there... my table neighbor... my cabin mate...

"And this is going to last another five times twenty-four hours!" Miss Nelly Underdown exclaimed the next day. "This is intolerable! I certainly hope they catch him."

Then, turning to me, she said, "Well, you, Mr. d'Andrézy, who are already on good terms with the captain, don't you know anything?"

I would have liked to know something to please Miss Nelly! She was one of those stunning creatures who, wherever they are, immediately take the most prominent position. Their beauty as much as their wealth dazzles. They have a following, admirers, enthusiasts.

Raised in Paris by a French mother, she was on her way to meet her father, the wealthy Underdown from Chicago. One of her friends, Lady Jerland, was accompanying her.

From the very first hour, I had put myself forward as a candidate for flirtation. But in the swift intimacy of the journey, her charm had unsettled me right away, and I felt a bit too overwhelmed for mere flirting when her large black eyes met mine. However, she seemed to welcome my attentions with a certain favor. She deigned to laugh at my witty remarks and showed interest in my anecdotes. A vague sympathy seemed to respond to the eagerness I displayed towards her.

The only rival who might have worried me was a rather handsome, elegant, reserved young man, whose taciturn demeanor she sometimes seemed to prefer over my more "outgoing" Parisian ways.

He was indeed part of the group of admirers surrounding Miss Nelly when she questioned me. We were on the deck, comfortably settled into rocking chairs. The storm from the previous day had cleared the sky. The hour was delightful.

—I don't know anything specific, Miss, I replied, but is it impossible for us to conduct our own investigation just as well as old Ganimard, Arsène Lupin's personal enemy, would?

—Oh! oh! you're getting ahead of yourself!

—In what way? Is the problem so complicated?

—Very complicated.

—That's because you're forgetting the elements we have to solve it.

—What elements?

—1° Lupin goes by the name Mr. R...

—That's a bit vague.

—2° He travels alone.

—If that peculiar detail is enough for you!

—3° He is blond.

—So what?

—So we just have to check the passenger list and proceed by elimination.

I had that list in my pocket. I took it out and skimmed through it.

—I first note that there are only thirteen people whose initial draws our attention.

—Only thirteen?

—In first class, yes. Of these thirteen Mr. R..., as you can confirm, nine are accompanied by women, children, or servants. That leaves four isolated individuals: the Marquis de Raverdan...

—Ambassador's secretary, Miss Nelly interrupted, I know him.

—Major Rawson...

—That's my uncle, someone said.

—Mr. Rivolta...

—Present, shouted one of us, an Italian whose face was obscured by a beautifully dark beard.

Miss Nelly burst out laughing.

—Sir is not exactly blond.

—So, I continued, we must conclude that the guilty party is the last one on the list.

—That is to say?

—That is to say, Mr. Rozaine. Does anyone know Mr. Rozaine?

We were silent. But Miss Nelly, addressing the taciturn young man whose constant presence near her troubled me, said:

— Well, Mr. Rozaine, aren't you going to respond?

Everyone turned their eyes toward him. He was blond.

I must admit, I felt a small shock deep inside me. And the awkward silence that hung over us indicated that the other attendees felt a similar kind of suffocation. It was absurd, really, because there was nothing in this gentleman's demeanor that would suggest any suspicion.

— Why am I not responding? he said, but because, given my name, my status as a lone traveler, and the color of my hair, I have already conducted a similar inquiry and arrived at the same conclusion. Therefore, I believe I should be detained.

He had a strange look on his face as he spoke those words. His thin lips, like two inflexible lines, thinned even more and paled. Veins of blood streaked across his eyes.

Certainly, he was joking. Yet his expression and demeanor impressed us. Naively, Miss Nelly asked:

— But you don't have an injury?

— That is true, he said, the injury is missing.

With a nervous gesture, he rolled up his cuff and revealed his arm. But immediately, an idea struck me. My eyes met Miss Nelly's: he had shown his left arm.

And indeed, I was about to point this out clearly when an incident diverted our attention. Lady Jerland, Miss Nelly's friend, came running in.

She was distraught. We rushed to her side, and it took her quite a while to stammer:

— My jewelry, my pearls!... they've taken everything!...

No, they hadn't taken everything, as we later learned; even more curious, they had made selections!

From the diamond star, the cabochon ruby pendant, the broken necklaces and bracelets, they had taken not the largest stones, but the finest, the most precious ones—those that seemed to hold the most value while taking up the least space. The settings lay there on the table. I saw them; we all saw them, stripped of their jewels like flowers from which the beautiful, sparkling, colorful petals had been torn away.

To carry out this task, it had been necessary, during the hour when Lady Jerland was having her tea, to break into the cabin door in broad daylight, in a busy hallway, find a small bag deliberately hidden at the bottom of a hat box, open it, and choose!

There was only one cry among us. There was only one opinion among all the passengers when the theft became known: it was Arsène Lupin. And indeed, it was clearly his complicated, mysterious, inconceivable... yet logical way, for while it would have been difficult to hide the bulky mass that the collection of jewels would have formed, how much easier it was with small items, independent of each other—pearls, emeralds, and sapphires.

And at dinner, this happened: to the right and left of Rozaine, the two seats remained empty. That evening, it was revealed that he had been summoned by the commander.

His arrest, which no one doubted, caused a genuine sense of relief. We could finally breathe again. That evening, we played little games. We danced. Miss Nelly, in particular, displayed a dazzling joy that made me realize that, while Rozaine's attentions may have pleased her at first, she hardly remembered them now. Her grace completely won me over. Around midnight, under the serene light of the moon, I professed my devotion to her with an emotion that did not seem to displease her.

But the next day, to everyone's astonishment, we learned that, the charges against him being insufficient, Rozaine was free.

The son of a prominent merchant from Bordeaux, he had presented perfectly valid papers. Moreover, his arms showed no signs of injury whatsoever.

"Papers! Birth certificates!" cried Rozaine's enemies, "but Arsène Lupin can provide you with as many as you want! As for the injury, either he didn't receive one… or he erased all traces of it!"

They were countered with the fact that at the time of the theft, Rozaine—this was proven—was walking on the deck. To which they responded:

"Does a man of Arsène Lupin's caliber need to witness the theft he commits?"

And then, aside from any external considerations, there was one point on which even the most skeptical could not argue: Who, besides Rozaine, traveled alone, was blond, and had a name starting with R? Who did the telegram refer to, if not Rozaine?

And when Rozaine boldly approached our group just minutes before lunch, Miss Nelly and Lady Jerland stood up and moved away.

It was indeed fear.

An hour later, a handwritten circular was passed around among the crew, sailors, and travelers of all classes: Mr. Louis Rozaine promised a sum of ten thousand francs to anyone who could unmask Arsène Lupin or find the owner of the stolen jewels.

—And if no one helps me against this bandit, Rozaine declared to the commander, I will deal with him myself.

Rozaine against Arsène Lupin, or rather, as the word spread, Arsène Lupin himself against Arsène Lupin, the struggle was certainly intriguing!

It lasted for two days. Rozaine was seen wandering back and forth, mingling with the crew, asking questions, snooping around. His shadow was spotted at night, lurking about.

Meanwhile, the commander exerted the utmost energy. From top to bottom, in every nook and cranny, the Provence was searched. They conducted searches of all the cabins, without exception, on the perfectly valid pretext that the stolen items could be hidden anywhere except in the cabin of the guilty party.

—We'll surely find something eventually, won't we? Miss Nelly asked me. No matter how clever he is, he can't make diamonds and pearls become invisible.

—But yes, I replied, or else we would have to search inside our hats, the linings of our jackets, and everything we're carrying.

And showing her my camera, a 9 X 12 that I never tired of using to photograph her in various poses:

—In a device no larger than this, don't you think there would be room for all Lady Jerland's jewels? They pretend to take pictures, and that's all it takes.

—But still, I've heard that there's no thief who doesn't leave some clue behind.

—There is one: Arsène Lupin.

—Why?

—Why? Because he doesn't just think about the theft he commits, but about all the circumstances that could expose him.

—At first, you were more confident.

—But since then, I have seen him in action.

—And what do you think?

—In my opinion, it's a waste of time.

And indeed, the investigations yielded no results, or at least, the one result they did yield did not match the overall effort: the commander's watch was stolen.

Furious, he redoubled his efforts and kept an even closer watch on Rozaine, with whom he had had several meetings. The next day, in a charming twist of irony, the watch was found among the false collars of the second-in-command.

All of this had an air of the miraculous, clearly showcasing the humorous style of Arsène Lupin, a thief, yes, but also a dabbler. He worked out of passion and vocation, certainly, but also for amusement. He gave the impression of a man who delights in the play he's putting on, and who, backstage, laughs heartily at his clever remarks and the situations he conjures up.

Clearly, he was an artist in his own right, and when I observed Rozaine, grim and stubborn, and thought about the double role that this curious character undoubtedly played, I could not speak of it without a certain admiration.

Now, on the night before last, the officer on duty heard moans coming from the darkest part of the deck. He approached. A man was lying there, his head wrapped in a very thick gray scarf, his wrists tied with a thin cord.

They freed him from his bonds. He was helped up, and care was given to him.

That man was Rozaine.

It was Rozaine who was attacked during one of his expeditions, knocked down and robbed. A business card pinned to his clothing bore the words: "Arsène Lupin gratefully accepts the ten thousand francs from Mr. Rozaine."

In reality, the stolen wallet contained twenty one-thousand-franc bills.

Naturally, the unfortunate man was accused of having staged this attack against himself. But aside from the fact that it would have been impossible for him to orchestrate such a scheme, it was established that the handwriting on the card was completely different from Rozaine's and, on the contrary, closely resembled that of Arsène Lupin, as reproduced in an old newspaper found on board.

Thus, Rozaine was no longer Arsène Lupin. Rozaine was Rozaine, the son of a merchant from Bordeaux! And the presence of Arsène Lupin was once again confirmed, and by such a formidable act!

It caused terror. No one dared to remain alone in their cabin, nor venture out alone to remote areas. Cautiously, people grouped together with those they trusted. Yet, even among the closest friends, there was an instinctive distrust. The threat did not come from a solitary individual, monitored and therefore less dangerous. Arsène Lupin, now, was... was everyone. Our excited imaginations attributed to him miraculous and limitless power. He was thought to be capable of adopting the most unexpected disguises, to be, in turn, the respectable Major Rawson, or the noble Marquis de Raverdan, or even—because no one stopped at the incriminating initial—even some well-known figure, with a wife, children, and servants.

The first wireless dispatches brought no news. At least, the commander did not share anything with us, and such silence did not reassure us.

Thus, the last day seemed endless. We lived in anxious anticipation of a disaster. This time, it would not be a theft, nor just a simple attack; it would be a crime, murder. We could not believe that Arsène Lupin would limit himself to these two insignificant thefts. As the absolute master of the ship, with the authorities rendered powerless, he could do whatever he wanted; everything was permitted to him, and he controlled both possessions and lives.

I must admit, these were delightful hours for me, as they earned me Miss Nelly's trust. Impressed by so many events and already of a worried nature, she instinctively sought protection and security by my side, which I was happy to offer her.

Deep down, I was grateful to Arsène Lupin. Wasn't he the one bringing us closer? Wasn't it thanks to him that I had the right to indulge in the most beautiful dreams? Dreams of love and less fanciful dreams—why not confess it? The Andrézy family has good Poitevin roots, but their coat of arms is somewhat tarnished, and it does not seem unworthy of a gentleman to think about restoring his name's lost luster.

And these dreams, I sensed, did not offend Nelly. Her smiling eyes allowed me to entertain them. The sweetness of her voice encouraged me to hope.

And until the very last moment, leaning on the railings, we stayed close to each other, while the line of the American coast sailed ahead of us.

We had interrupted the searches. We were waiting. From the first moments to the hold where the emigrants were bustling, we were waiting for the supreme moment when the unsolvable enigma would finally be explained. Who was Arsène Lupin? Under what name, under what mask was the famous Arsène Lupin hiding?

And that supreme moment arrived. Even if I were to live a hundred years, I will never forget the smallest detail.

—You look so pale, Miss Nelly, I said to my companion who was leaning on my arm, feeling faint.

—And you! she replied, oh! you have changed so much!

—Just think! this moment is thrilling, and I am so happy to experience it with you, Miss Nelly. It seems to me that your memory will linger sometimes...

She wasn't listening, breathless and feverish. The gangway was lowered. But before we had the freedom to cross it, people boarded the ship—customs officers, men in uniform, postal workers.

Miss Nelly stammered:

—They would realize that Arsène Lupin escaped during the crossing, and I wouldn't be surprised.

—He may have preferred death to dishonor, plunging into the Atlantic rather than being captured.

—Don't laugh, she said, annoyed.

Suddenly I started, and as she questioned me, I said:

—Do you see that old little man standing at the end of the gangway?

—With an umbrella and an olive-green coat?

—That's Ganimard.

—Ganimard?

—Yes, the famous detective, the one who swore that Arsène Lupin would be caught by his own hand. Ah! I understand why there hadn't been any information from this side of the Ocean. Ganimard was here! and he prefers that no one meddles in his little affairs.

—Then Arsène Lupin is sure to be caught?

"Who knows? Ganimard has never seen him, it seems, except in disguise. Unless he knows his alias..."

"Ah!" she said, with that slightly cruel curiosity of a woman, "if only I could witness the arrest!"

"Let's be patient. Certainly Arsène Lupin has already noticed the presence of his enemy. He will prefer to leave among the last, when the old man's eye is tired."

The disembarkation began. Leaning on his umbrella, looking indifferent, Ganimard seemed not to pay attention to the crowd pressing between the two railings. I noted that an officer on board, stationed behind him, was giving him information from time to time.

Marquis de Raverdan, Major Rawson, the Italian Rivolta, passed by, and others, many others... And I spotted Rozaine approaching.

Poor Rozaine! He didn't seem to have recovered from his misfortunes!

"It might be him after all," Miss Nelly said to me... "What do you think?"

"I think it would be quite interesting to have Ganimard and Rozaine in the same photograph. Why don't you take my camera? I'm so loaded down."

I handed it to her, but it was too late for her to use it. Rozaine passed by. The officer leaned in to Ganimard's ear, who shrugged slightly, and Rozaine moved on.

But then, my God, who was Arsène Lupin?

"Yes," she said aloud, "who is he?"

There were only about twenty people left. She watched each of them in turn, with the confused fear that he might not be among those twenty.

I said to her:

"We can't wait any longer."

She stepped forward. I followed her. But we hadn't taken ten steps when Ganimard blocked our path.

"Well, what is it?" I exclaimed.

"Just a moment, sir, what is your hurry?"

"I'm accompanying the young lady."

"One moment," he repeated in a more commanding voice.

He stared at me deeply, then said, looking me straight in the eyes:

"Arsène Lupin, isn't it?"

I began to laugh.

"No, Bernard d'Andrézy, quite simply."

"Bernard d'Andrézy died three years ago in Macedonia."

"If Bernard d'Andrézy were dead, I wouldn't be here. And that is not the case. Here are my papers."

"These are his. How you got them is something I will enjoy explaining to you."

"But you are crazy! Arsène Lupin boarded under the name R."

"Yes, just another trick of yours, a false lead that you sent them on over there. Ah! You are quite something, my friend. But this time, luck has turned. Now, Lupin, show yourself a good sport."

I hesitated for a second. Suddenly, he struck me on the right forearm. I let out a cry of pain. He had hit the still-healing wound that the telegram had mentioned.

Well, I had to resign myself. I turned to Miss Nelly. She was listening, pale and unsteady.

Her gaze met mine, then dropped to the Kodak I had handed her. She made a sudden gesture, and I felt, I was certain that she suddenly understood everything. Yes, it was there, between the narrow walls of black sorrow, in the small object I had taken the precaution of placing in her hands before Ganimard arrested me; it was indeed there that the twenty thousand francs from Rozaine, the pearls and diamonds of Lady Jerland were located.

Ah! I swear, at that solemn moment, as Ganimard and two of his accomplices surrounded me, everything was indifferent to me—my arrest, the hostility of the people, everything—except for this: the decision that Miss Nelly would make regarding what I had entrusted to her.

Even if I had that material and decisive proof against me, I didn't even think to fear it. But would Miss Nelly decide to provide that proof?

Would she betray me? Would I be lost because of her? Would she act like an enemy who does not forgive, or like a woman who remembers and whose disdain softens with a bit of understanding, a touch of involuntary sympathy?

She passed in front of me, and I greeted her with a very slight nod, without a word. Blending in with the other travelers, she headed towards the gangway, my Kodak in hand.

Surely, I thought, she doesn't dare to do it in public. It will be in an hour, in a moment, that she will give it.

But, when she reached the middle of the gangway, with a feigned clumsiness, she let it fall into the water, between the quay wall and the ship's side.

Then, I saw her walk away.

Her pretty silhouette vanished into the crowd, reappeared, and then disappeared again. It was over, finished forever.

For a moment, I remained still, both sad and filled with a gentle tenderness, then I sighed, to Ganimard's great astonishment:

—It's a pity, after all, not to be an honest man…

This is how one winter evening, Arsène Lupin told me the story of his arrest. The chance incidents, which I will someday recount, had woven a bond between us… shall I say of friendship? Yes, I dare to believe that Arsène Lupin honors me with some friendship, and that it is out of friendship that he sometimes shows up at my place unexpectedly, bringing with him, into the quiet of my study, his youthful cheerfulness, the radiance of his passionate life, and his good humor of a man for whom destiny has only favors and smiles.

His portrait? How could I create it? Twenty times I have seen Arsène Lupin, and twenty times a different being has appeared to me… or rather the same being whose image would have been reflected in twenty mirrors, each distorting it, each with its own particular eyes, its unique facial shape, its distinct gestures, silhouette, and character.

—As for myself, he told me, I no longer know exactly who I am. In a mirror, I no longer recognize myself.

A jest, of course, and a paradox, but a truth regarding those who encounter him and are unaware of his infinite resources, his patience, his art of disguise, and his extraordinary ability to transform even the proportions of his face and alter the very relationship between his features.

—Why, he continued, should I have a fixed appearance? Why not avoid the danger of always having the same personality? My actions define me well enough.

And he emphasizes with a hint of pride:

—All the better if one can never say with complete certainty: Here is Arsène Lupin. The important thing is that one can say without fear of error: Arsène Lupin did this.

These are some of those actions, some of those adventures that I am trying to reconstruct, based on the confidences he kindly shared with me on certain winter evenings, in the silence of my study…

CHAPTER TWO
ARSÈNE LUPIN IN PRISON

No tourist worthy of the name is unfamiliar with the banks of the Seine, and no one can miss the strange little feudal castle of Malaquis, so proudly perched on its rock in the middle of the river, when traveling from the ruins of Jumièges to the ruins of Saint-Wandrille. An arch of a bridge connects it to the road. The base of its dark towers merges with the granite that supports it, an enormous block detached from some unknown mountain and thrown there by some formidable upheaval. All around, the calm waters of the great river play among the reeds, and wagtails tremble on the damp crest of the pebbles.

The history of Malaquis is as rough as its name, and as grim as its silhouette. It has been nothing but battles, sieges, assaults, plunder, and massacres. Around the firesides in the Pays de Caux, people shudder as they recall the crimes committed there. Mysterious legends are recounted. There is talk of the famous underground passage that once led to the abbey of Jumièges and to the manor of Agnès Sorel, the beautiful mistress of Charles VII.

In this ancient lair of heroes and bandits resides Baron Nathan Cahorn, known as Baron Satan, as he was once called at the Stock Exchange, where he amassed his wealth rather too quickly. The lords of Malaquis, now ruined, had to sell him their ancestral home for a mere pittance. He has installed his remarkable collections of furniture and paintings, ceramics, and carved wood there. He lives there alone, with three old servants. No one ever enters. No one has ever gazed upon the three Rubens he possesses, his two Watteaus, his lectern by Jean Goujon, and so many other wonders wrested from the richest patrons at public auctions with the stroke of a banknote.

Baron Satan is afraid. He is not afraid for himself, but for the treasures he has accumulated with such tenacity and the insight of an amateur that even the shrewdest merchants cannot claim to have misled him. He loves his trinkets. He loves them fiercely, like a miser; jealously, like a lover.

Every day at sunset, the four iron-clad doors that control both ends of the bridge and the entrance to the courtyard are closed and locked. At the slightest disturbance, electric bells would ring out in the silence. On the Seine side, there is nothing to fear: the rock rises steeply.

One Friday in September, the postman arrived as usual at the outpost. And, following the daily routine, it was the baron who cracked open the heavy door.

He scrutinized the man as thoroughly as if he didn't already know this cheerful face and those mischievous peasant eyes for years, and the man said to him, laughing:

—It's still me, Mr. Baron. I'm not someone else who took my smock and cap.

—Can one ever be sure? murmured Cahorn.

The postman handed him a stack of newspapers. Then he added:

—And now, Mr. Baron, there's something new.

—Something new?

—A letter... and it's registered, too.

Isolated, without friends or anyone who cared about him, the baron never received letters, and immediately this seemed to him an ominous event that he should be concerned about. Who was this mysterious correspondent trying to reach him in his seclusion?

—You need to sign, Mr. Baron.

He signed with a grunt. Then he took the letter, waited until the postman had turned the corner, and after pacing back and forth for a moment, leaned against the bridge's parapet and tore open the envelope. Inside was a sheet of squared paper with this handwritten heading: Prison de la Santé, Paris. He looked at the signature: Arsène Lupin. Stunned, he read:

"Dear Baron,

"There is a painting by Philippe de Champaigne of excellent quality in the gallery that connects your two salons, and I am very fond of it. Your Rubens also appeal to me, as does your smaller Watteau. In the right salon, I note the Louis XIII sideboard, the Beauvais tapestries, the Empire guéridon signed by Jacob, and the Renaissance cabinet. In the left salon, the entire display of jewelry and miniatures.

"For this occasion, I will settle for these items, which I believe will be easy to dispose of. Therefore, I kindly ask you to have them properly packed and sent in my name (post paid) to the Batignolles train station within eight days... otherwise, I will personally arrange for their relocation during the night of Wednesday, September 27 to Thursday, September 28. And, of course, I will not limit myself to the aforementioned items.

"Please excuse the small inconvenience I am causing you, and accept the expression of my respectful consideration.

"ARSÈNE LUPIN."

"P.S.—Above all, do not send me the largest Watteau. Although you paid thirty thousand francs for it at the Auction House, it is only a copy, the original having been burned by Barras one orgiastic night under the Directory. Refer to the unpublished Memoirs of Garat.

"I am also not interested in the Louis XV lady's desk, as its authenticity seems questionable to me."

This letter shook Baron Cahorn to his core. Signed by anyone else, it would have alarmed him greatly, but signed by Arsène Lupin!

As a regular reader of newspapers, well-informed about everything happening in the world of theft and crime, he was fully aware of the exploits of the infernal burglar. Certainly, he knew that Lupin, arrested in America by his nemesis Ganimard, was indeed incarcerated and that his trial was underway—with what difficulty!—

But he also knew that anything could be expected from him. Moreover, this precise knowledge of the castle, the arrangement of the paintings and furniture, was a most formidable clue. Who had informed him about things that no one had seen?

The baron looked up and gazed at the fierce silhouette of the Malaquis, its steep pedestal, the deep water surrounding it, and shrugged his shoulders. No, there was definitely no danger. No one in the world could penetrate the inviolable sanctuary of his collections.

No one, perhaps, but Arsène Lupin? For Arsène Lupin, do doors, drawbridges, or walls even exist? What good are the most cleverly devised obstacles and the most skillful precautions if Arsène Lupin has set his sights on a particular goal?

That very evening, he wrote to the public prosecutor in Rouen. He sent the threatening letter and requested help and protection.

The response was swift: the individual named Arsène Lupin was currently detained at La Santé, under close surveillance, and unable to write; thus, the letter could only be the work of a trickster. Everything suggested this—logic, common sense, and the reality of the facts. However, out of an excess of caution, an expert had been commissioned to examine the handwriting, and the expert declared that, despite certain similarities, this handwriting was not that of the detainee.

"Despite certain similarities"—the baron clung to those three alarming words, in which he saw an admission of doubt that alone should have been enough for the justice system to intervene. His fears intensified. He kept rereading the letter. "I will personally arrange for the move." And that precise date: the night of Wednesday, September 27 to Thursday, September 28!...

Suspicious and taciturn, he had not dared to confide in his servants, whose loyalty he felt might not withstand any test. However, for the first time in years, he felt the need to speak, to seek advice. Abandoned by the justice of his country, he no longer hoped to defend himself with his own resources, and he came close to going to Paris to implore the assistance of some former police officer.

Two days passed. On the third day, while reading his newspapers, he was jolted with joy. Le Réveil de Caudebec published this brief article:

"We are pleased to have in our midst, for almost three weeks now, Chief Inspector Ganimard, one of the veterans of the Security Service. Mr. Ganimard, whose arrest of Arsène Lupin, his latest feat, has earned him a European reputation, is resting from his long labors by fishing for gudgeon and bleak."

Ganimard! There's the assistant that Baron Cahorn was looking for! Who better than the cunning and patient Ganimard to thwart Lupin's plans?

The baron did not hesitate. Six kilometers separate the castle from the small town of Caudebec. He crossed them with a lively step, a man energized by the hope of salvation.

After several unsuccessful attempts to find out the address of the chief inspector, he made his way to the offices of the Réveil, located in the middle of the quay. There, he found the writer of the brief article who, moving closer to the window, exclaimed:

—Ganimard? But you're sure to find him along the quay, rod in hand. That's where we first met, and I happened to read his name engraved on his fishing rod. Look, the little old man you can see over there, under the trees in the promenade.

—In a frock coat and straw hat?

—Exactly! Ah! A funny character, not very talkative and rather gruff.

Five minutes later, the baron approached the famous Ganimard, introduced himself, and tried to strike up a conversation. When that failed, he straightforwardly tackled the issue and laid out his case.

The other listened, motionless, without taking his eyes off the fish he was watching, then turned his head towards him, sizing him up from head to toe with a profound look of pity, and said:

—Sir, it is not customary to warn people when one intends to rob them. Arsène Lupin, in particular, does not make such blunders.

—However...

—Sir, if I had the slightest doubt, believe me, the pleasure of getting back at dear Lupin would outweigh any other consideration. Unfortunately, that young man is behind bars.

—What if he escapes?…

—No one escapes from La Santé.

—But he…

—He is no different from anyone else.

—However…

"Well, if he escapes, so much the better; I'll catch him again. In the meantime, sleep soundly, and don't frighten that little fish any further."

The conversation was over. The baron returned home, somewhat reassured by Ganimard's carefree attitude. He checked the locks, watched the servants, and another forty-eight hours passed during which he almost convinced himself that his fears were unfounded. No, definitely, as Ganimard had said, you don't warn people you intend to rob.

The date was approaching. On the morning of Tuesday, the day before the 27th, nothing special happened. But at three o'clock, a boy rang the bell. He brought a telegram.

"No package at the Batignolles station. Prepare everything for tomorrow night.

"ARSÈNE."

Once again, panic set in, to the point that he wondered if he should give in to Arsène Lupin's demands.

He ran to Caudebec. Ganimard was fishing in the same spot, sitting on a folding chair. Without a word, he handed him the telegram.

"And then?" the inspector asked.

"And then? But it's for tomorrow!"

"What?"

"The burglary! The looting of my collections!"

Ganimard put down his fishing line, turned to him, and, arms crossed over his chest, exclaimed impatiently, "Oh, do you really think I'm going to get involved in such a ridiculous story?"

"What compensation do you want to spend the night at the castle from the 27th to the 28th of September?"

"Not a penny, leave me alone."

"Name your price; I'm rich, extremely rich."

The bluntness of the offer took Ganimard aback, but he replied more calmly, "I'm here on leave, and I don't have the right to get involved..."

"No one will know. I promise, no matter what happens, to keep it a secret."

"Oh! Nothing will happen."

"Well then, let's see, three thousand francs; is that enough?"

The inspector took a puff of tobacco, thought for a moment, and then said:

—Fine. However, I must honestly tell you that this is money thrown out the window.

—I don't care.

—In that case... And after all, who knows with that devil Lupin! He must have a whole gang at his command... Are you sure about your servants?

—Well...

—Then, let's not rely on them. I will send a telegram to two of my friends who will provide us with more security... And now, hurry up, we can't be seen together. See you tomorrow, around nine o'clock.

***

The next day, the date set by Arsène Lupin, Baron Cahorn donned his gear, polished his weapons, and walked around the grounds of Malaquis. Nothing unusual caught his eye.

That evening, at eight-thirty, he dismissed his servants. They lived in a wing facing the road, but set back a bit, at the far end of the castle. Once alone, he quietly opened all four doors. After a moment, he heard footsteps approaching.

Ganimard introduced his two assistants, big, solid guys with bull-like necks and powerful hands, and then asked for some explanations. Realizing the layout of the place, he carefully locked and barricaded all the entrances that could lead into the threatened rooms. He inspected the walls, lifted the tapestries, and finally positioned his agents in the central gallery.

—No foolishness, got it? We're not here to sleep. At the first sign of trouble, open the windows to the courtyard and call me. Also be careful by the water. Ten meters of sheer cliff—devils like them aren't scared of that.

He locked them in, took the keys, and said to the baron:

—And now, to our posts.

He had chosen a small room carved into the thickness of the enclosing walls, situated between the two main doors, which had once served as the watchman's quarters. A peephole opened onto the bridge, another onto the courtyard. In one corner, there was what looked like an opening to a well.

—You did tell me, Baron, that this well was the only entrance to the underground tunnels, and that, for as long as anyone can remember, it has been blocked up?

—Yes.

—So, unless there is another exit known only to Arsène Lupin, which seems a bit unlikely, we can rest easy.

He aligned three chairs, settled in comfortably, lit his pipe, and sighed:

—Honestly, Baron, I must really want to add a floor to the little house where I plan to spend my days, to take on such a basic task. I'll tell the story to my friend Lupin; he'll be doubled over with laughter.

The Baron was not laughing. With his ear to the ground, he was questioning the silence with increasing concern. From time to time, he leaned over the well, peering anxiously into the gaping hole.

Eleven o'clock, midnight, one o'clock struck.

Suddenly, he grabbed Ganimard's arm, waking him up with a start.

—Do you hear that?

—Yes.

—What is it?

—It's me snoring!

—No, listen...

—Ah! Right, it's the horn of a car.

—So what?

—Well, it's unlikely that Lupin would use a car as a battering ram to demolish your castle. So, Baron, if I were you, I would sleep... as I'm about to honorably do again. Goodnight.

That was the only alarm. Ganimard was able to resume his interrupted nap, and the Baron heard nothing more than his loud and regular snoring.

At dawn, they emerged from their cell. A great serene peace, the peace of morning by the cool water, enveloped the castle. Cahorn was radiant with joy, while Ganimard remained calm as they ascended the staircase. No noise. Nothing suspicious.

—What did I tell you, Baron? In the end, I shouldn't have accepted... I am ashamed...

He took the keys and entered the gallery.

On two chairs, hunched over with their arms dangling, the two agents were asleep.

—Thunder of the name of a dog! grumbled the inspector.

At that moment, the baron let out a cry:

—The paintings!... the credenza!...

He stammered, gasping, his hand pointing towards the empty spots, towards the bare walls where nails stuck out, where useless ropes hung. The Watteau, gone! The Rubens, taken! The tapestries, unhooked! The display cases, emptied of their jewels!

—And my Louis XVI candelabras!... and the Regent's chandelier!... and my twelfth-century Madonna!...

He ran from one place to another, frantic and desperate. He recalled his purchase prices, added up the losses he had suffered, accumulating figures, all jumbled together, in indistinct words, in unfinished sentences. He stomped his feet, convulsed, mad with rage and pain. He looked like a ruined man who had nothing left but to blow his brains out.

If anything could have consoled him, it would have been to see Ganimard's astonishment. Unlike the baron, the inspector did not move. He seemed petrified, and with a vacant gaze, he examined the scene. The windows? Closed. The door locks? Intact. No breach in the ceiling. No hole in the floor. Everything was in order. It must have all been carried out methodically, according to a relentless and logical plan.

—Arsène Lupin... Arsène Lupin, he murmured, overwhelmed.

Suddenly, he lunged at the two agents, as if a wave of anger had finally taken hold of him, and he shoved them furiously while hurling insults. They didn't wake up at all!

—Good heavens, he said, could it be that...

He leaned over them and observed each one closely: they were asleep, but it was not a natural sleep.

He said to the baron:

—They've been put to sleep.

—But by whom?

—Well, him, of course!... or his gang, but led by him. This is his style. The mark is unmistakably there.

—In that case, I'm doomed, nothing can be done.

—Nothing can be done.

—But this is outrageous, it's monstrous.

—File a complaint.

—What good would that do?

—Well, give it a try... justice has its resources...

—Justice! But you can see for yourself... Look, right now, when you could be searching for a clue, discovering something, you're not even moving.

—Discover something with Arsène Lupin! My dear sir, Arsène Lupin never leaves anything behind! There's no randomness with Arsène

Lupin ! I'm starting to wonder if he didn't get himself caught on purpose by me in America !

—Then I must give up my paintings, everything ! But it's the pearls from my collection that he stole from me. I would give a fortune to get them back. If nothing can be done against him, let him state his price !

Ganimard looked at him intently.

—That's a sensible statement. You won't take it back ?

—No, no, no. But why ?

—I have an idea.

—What idea ?

—We'll talk about it if the investigation doesn't yield results… Just, not a word from me, if you want me to succeed.

He added under his breath:

—And honestly, I have no cause to brag.

The two agents gradually regained consciousness, looking dazed like those awakening from a hypnotic sleep. They opened their eyes in surprise, trying to understand. When Ganimard questioned them, they remembered nothing.

—However, you must have seen someone ?

—No.

—Think hard.

—No, no.

—And you didn't drink ?

They thought for a moment, and one of them replied:

—Yes, I drank a little water.

—From this carafe?

—Yes.

—Me too, declared the second.

Ganimard picked it up and tasted it. It had no special taste or smell.

—Well then, he said, we're wasting our time. You don't solve the problems posed by Arsène Lupin in five minutes. But, by thunder! I swear I will catch him again. He wins this round. The next one's mine!

That same day, a complaint of theft was filed by Baron de Cahorn against Arsène Lupin, who was held at La Santé!

* * *

The baron often regretted this complaint when he saw Malaquis handed over to the gendarmes, the prosecutor, the investigating judge, the journalists, and all the curious people who insert themselves where they shouldn't be.

The case was already captivating public opinion. It unfolded under such unusual circumstances, and the name Arsène Lupin stirred the imagination to such an extent that the most fanciful stories filled the columns of newspapers and found credence with the public.

But the initial letter from Arsène Lupin, which was published by L'Écho de France (and no one ever knew who had shared the text), in which Baron Cahorn was brazenly warned of the threat he faced, caused considerable excitement. Immediately, fantastic explanations were proposed. The existence of the famous underground tunnels was recalled. And the influenced authorities pushed their investigations in that direction.

They searched the castle from top to bottom. They questioned every stone. They studied the woodwork and the fireplaces, the frames of the mirrors, and the beams of the ceilings. By the light of torches, they examined the vast cellars where the lords of Malaquis once stored their ammunition and supplies. They probed the depths of the rock. It was in vain. Not a single trace of a tunnel was found. There was no secret passage.

"That's fine," people replied from all sides, "but furniture and paintings do not just vanish like ghosts. They leave through doors and windows, and the people who take them enter and exit through doors and windows as well. Who are these people? How did they get in? And how did they leave?"

The Rouen authorities, convinced of their impotence, sought help from Parisian agents. Mr. Dudouis, the head of the Sûreté, sent his best detectives from the iron brigade. He himself spent forty-eight hours at Malaquis. He was no more successful.

It was then that he summoned Chief Inspector Ganimard, whose services he had often come to appreciate.

Ganimard listened silently to his superior's instructions, then, shaking his head, he said:

—I believe we are on the wrong track by insisting on searching the castle. The solution lies elsewhere.

—And where exactly?

—With Arsène Lupin.

—With Arsène Lupin! To assume that is to acknowledge his involvement.

—I do acknowledge it. Moreover, I consider it certain.

—Come now, Ganimard, that's absurd. Arsène Lupin is in prison.

—Arsène Lupin is indeed in prison, I grant you that. He is being watched, I agree. But even if he were shackled, ropes around his wrists, and a gag in his mouth, I wouldn't change my mind.

—And why this stubbornness?

—Because, alone, Arsène Lupin is capable of devising a scheme of this magnitude, and doing so in a way that it succeeds... just as it has succeeded.

—Words, Ganimard!

—Which are realities. But let's not look for secret passages, stones turning on a pivot, and other nonsense of that sort. Our individual doesn't use such outdated methods. He is of today, or rather of tomorrow.

—And what is your conclusion?

—I conclude by clearly asking for your permission to spend an hour with him.

—In his cell?

—Yes. Upon returning from America, we had excellent rapport during the crossing, and I dare say he has some sympathy for the one who managed to catch him. If he can inform me without compromising himself, he won't hesitate to spare me an unnecessary trip.

It was a little past noon when Ganimard was introduced into Arsène Lupin's cell. Lupin, lying on his bed, lifted his head and let out a cry of joy.

—Ah! Now, that's a real surprise. My dear Ganimard, here!

—It's me.

—I wished for many things in the retreat I chose... but none more passionately than to host you here.

—Too kind of you.

—No, no, I hold you in the highest regard.

—I am proud of that.

—I have always claimed: Ganimard is our best detective. He's almost —see how candid I am!—almost as good as Sherlock Holmes. But truly, I'm sorry to offer you only this stool. And no refreshments! Not even a glass of beer! Forgive me, I'm just passing through.

Ganimard sat down with a smile, and the prisoner continued, happy to talk:

—My God, how glad I am to rest my eyes on the face of an honest man! I'm so tired of all those faces of spies and informants who go through my pockets and my modest cell ten times a day to make sure I'm not planning an escape. Goodness, how the government is attached to me!...

—He's right.

—But no! I would be so happy if they would just let me live in my little corner!

—With other people's rents.

—Isn't that so? It would be so simple! But I'm rambling, I'm saying nonsense, and you might be in a hurry. Let's get to the point, Ganimard! What brings you the honor of a visit?

—The Cahorn case, Ganimard declared straightforwardly.

—Hold on a second... I have so many cases! Let me first find the Cahorn case file in my mind... Ah! There it is. Cahorn case, Malaquis Castle, Seine-Inférieure... Two Rubens, a Watteau, and a few minor items.

—Minor!

—Oh, my word, all of that is of little importance. There's more! But it's enough that the case interests you... So go ahead, Ganimard.

—Should I explain where we stand with the investigation?

—Unnecessary. I read this morning's newspapers. I'll even go so far as to say you're not making much progress.

—That's precisely the reason I'm turning to your kindness.

—Entirely at your service.

—First of all, was the matter handled properly by you?

—From A to Z.

—The notification letter? The telegram?

—Are from your servant. I should even have the receipts somewhere.

Arsène opened the drawer of a small white wooden table, which, along with the bed and the stool, made up all the furniture in his cell, took out two scraps of paper, and handed them to Ganimard.

—Ah! But, exclaimed Ganimard, I thought you were being held in custody and searched for no reason. Yet you read the newspapers and collect postal receipts...

—Well! Those people are so foolish! They rip the lining of my jacket, explore the soles of my boots, examine the walls of this room, but not one of them would think that Arsène Lupin could be foolish enough to choose such an easy hiding place. That's exactly what I was counting on.

Ganimard, amused, exclaimed:

—What a funny fellow you are! You perplex me. Come on, tell me about the adventure.

—Oh! oh! How bold of you! To share all my secrets with you... to reveal my little tricks... That's quite serious.

—Have I been wrong to rely on your willingness to cooperate?

—No, Ganimard, and since you insist...

Arsène Lupin paced back and forth in his room a couple of times, then stopped:

—What do you think of my letter to the baron?

—I think you wanted to entertain yourself, to impress a little.

—Ah! There you are, putting on a show! Well, I assure you, Ganimard, that I thought you were stronger than this. Am I really going to dwell on such trivialities, I, Arsène Lupin? Would I have written this letter if I could have robbed the baron without it? But you and the others must understand that this letter is the essential starting point, the spring that set the whole machine in motion. Now, let's proceed in order, and let's prepare together, if you'd like, for the burglary of the Malaquis.

—I'm listening.

—So, let's suppose there's a castle that is rigorously closed, barricaded, just like the one belonging to Baron Cahorn. Am I going to give up and abandon treasures I covet just because the castle that holds them is inaccessible?

—Obviously not.

—Am I going to attempt an assault as I did in the past, leading a band of adventurers?

—Childish!

—Am I going to sneak in?

—Impossible.

—There remains one method, the only one in my opinion, which is to get invited by the owner of the said castle.

—That's an original approach.

—And how easy it is! Let's suppose one day that the owner receives a letter warning him about a plot against him by someone named Arsène Lupin, a notorious burglar. What will he do?

—He'll send the letter to the prosecutor.

—Who will laugh at him, since Lupin is currently behind bars. So, the poor man will panic and be ready to seek help from anyone, right?

—That's beyond doubt.

—And if he happens to read in a newspaper that a famous police officer is vacationing in the nearby area…

—He will go to that police officer.

—You said it. But on the other hand, let's assume that in anticipation of this inevitable move, Arsène Lupin asked one of his most skilled friends to settle in Caudebec, to make contact with a writer from the Réveil, the newspaper to which the baron is subscribed, and to suggest that he is such a person, the famous policeman. What will happen then?

—The writer will announce in the Réveil the presence of the said policeman in Caudebec.

—Perfect, and there are two possibilities: either the fish—I mean Cahorn—doesn't take the bait, and then nothing happens. Or, and this is the more likely scenario, he comes rushing in, all excited. And so my Cahorn ends up begging one of my friends for help against me!

—More and more original.

—Of course, the faux-policeman initially refuses to help. Then, a message from Arsène Lupin arrives. The baron is terrified and pleads once again with my friend, offering him a considerable sum to ensure his safety. The friend agrees, brings along two tough guys from our gang, who, at night, while Cahorn is being held by his protector, move out a number of items through the window and lower them using ropes into a nice little boat hired for the occasion. It's as simple as Lupin.

—And it's absolutely marvelous, exclaimed Ganimard, and I cannot praise enough the boldness of the idea and the ingenuity of the details. But I hardly see any policeman notable enough for his name to have attracted or suggested to the baron in such a way.

—There is one, and only one.

—Who?

—The most famous one, the personal enemy of Arsène Lupin, in short, Inspector Ganimard.

—Me!

—You yourself, Ganimard. And here's the delightful part: if you go over there and the baron decides to talk, you'll end up discovering that your duty is to stop yourself, just like you stopped me in America. Ha! The irony is amusing: I have Ganimard arrested by Ganimard!

Arsène Lupin laughed heartily. The inspector, somewhat annoyed, bit his lips. The joke didn't seem to him to warrant such bursts of joy.

The arrival of a guard gave him the chance to compose himself. The man brought the meal that Arsène Lupin, as a special favor, had ordered from the nearby restaurant. After placing the tray on the table, he stepped back. Arsène settled down, broke his bread, ate two or three bites, and continued:

—But rest assured, my dear Ganimard, you won't be going over there. I'm about to reveal something that will astonish you: the Cahorn case is about to be closed.

—What!

—About to be closed, I tell you.

—Come now, I just left the chief of police.

—And so? Does Mr. Dudouis know more than I do about what concerns me? You'll learn that Ganimard—excuse me—that the pseudo-Ganimard has remained on very good terms with the baron. The latter, and this is the main reason he hasn't confessed anything, has entrusted him with the very delicate mission of negotiating a deal with me, and at this moment, for a certain sum, it's likely that the baron has regained possession of his precious trinkets. In return, he will withdraw his complaint. So, no more theft. Therefore, the prosecution will have no choice but to drop...

Ganimard looked at the detainee in astonishment.

—And how do you know all this?

—I just received the telegram I was waiting for.

—You just received a telegram?

—Just a moment, my dear friend. Out of politeness, I didn't want to read it in your presence. But if you allow me...

—You're mocking me, Lupin.

—Please, my dear friend, gently crack this soft-boiled egg. You will see for yourself that I am not mocking you.

Mechanically, Ganimard complied and broke the egg with the edge of a knife. A cry of surprise escaped him. The empty shell contained a piece of blue paper. At Arsène's request, he unfolded it. It was a telegram, or rather a part of a telegram from which the postal details had been torn away. He read:

"Agreement reached. One hundred thousand francs delivered. All is well."

—One hundred thousand francs? he said.

—Yes, one hundred thousand francs! It's not much, but times are tough... And my overhead costs are so high! If you only knew my budget... a big-city budget!

Ganimard stood up. His bad mood had lifted. He thought for a few seconds, taking in the whole situation to try to discover its weak point. Then he spoke in a tone that clearly revealed his admiration as a connoisseur:

—Fortunately, there aren't dozens like you; otherwise, it would be time to close up shop.

Arsène Lupin assumed a modest demeanor and replied:

—Oh! One had to find a way to entertain oneself, occupy one's leisure... especially since the plan could only succeed if I were in prison.

—What! exclaimed Ganimard, your trial, your defense, the investigation—none of this is enough to keep you entertained?

—No, because I have decided not to attend my trial.

—Oh! oh!

Arsène Lupin calmly repeated:

—I will not attend my trial.

—Really!

—Ah! My dear, do you think I'm going to rot on this damp straw? You insult me. Arsène Lupin only stays in prison as long as he chooses, not a minute longer.

—It might have been wiser to start by not entering at all, the inspector replied with an ironic tone.

—Oh! Are you mocking me? Do you remember that you had the honor of arresting me? Know this, my respectable friend: no one, neither you nor anyone else, could have laid a hand on me if a much greater interest hadn't compelled me at that critical moment.

—You astonish me.

—A woman was looking at me, Ganimard, and I loved her. Do you understand everything that comes with being looked at by a woman you love? The rest mattered little to me, I swear. And that's why I am here.

—For quite some time now, if I may point that out.

—I wanted to forget, at first. Don't laugh: the adventure was delightful, and I still cherish the tender memory... And then, I am somewhat neurasthenic! Life is so feverish these days! At certain times, one must do what is called a cure of isolation. This place is perfect for such regimes. They conduct the health cure here in all its rigor.

—Arsène Lupin, Ganimard observed, you're making a fool of me.

—Ganimard, Lupin affirmed, today is Friday. Next Wednesday, I will come smoke my cigar at your place, on Rue Pergolèse, at four in the afternoon.

—Arsène Lupin, I will be waiting for you.

They shook hands like two good friends who appreciate each other's worth, and the old policeman headed toward the door.

—Ganimard!

He turned around.

—What is it?

—Ganimard, you're forgetting your watch.

—My watch?

—Yes, it's gotten lost in my pocket.

He handed it back while apologizing.

—Forgive me... a bad habit... But that doesn't justify taking away your pocket watch just because they took mine. Besides, I have a stopwatch here that I can't complain about, which fully meets my needs.

He pulled a large gold watch from the drawer, thick and comfortable, adorned with a heavy chain.

—And where does this one come from? asked Ganimard.

Arsène Lupin casually examined the initials.

—J. B... Who on earth could that be?... Ah! yes, I remember, Jules Bouvier, my examining magistrate, a charming man...

CHAPTER THREE
THE ESCAPE OF ARSÈNE LUPIN

At the moment when Arsène Lupin, having finished his meal, took out a beautiful cigar with a gold band from his pocket and examined it with satisfaction, the door of the cell opened. He barely had time to toss it into the drawer and step away from the table. The guard entered; it was time for the walk.

—I was waiting for you, my dear friend, exclaimed Lupin, always in good spirits.

They went outside. They had hardly disappeared around the corner of the corridor when two men entered the cell and began a thorough examination. One was Inspector Dieuzy, the other Inspector Folenfant.

They wanted to put an end to it. There was no doubt: Arsène Lupin was still in communication with the outside world and was in contact with his associates. Just the day before, the Grand Journal published these lines addressed to his judicial collaborator:

"Sir,

"In an article published recently, you expressed yourself about me in terms that are utterly unjustifiable. A few days before my trial begins, I will come to demand an explanation from you.

"Best regards,

"ARSÈNE LUPIN."

The writing was indeed by Arsène Lupin. So he sent letters. Therefore, he received them. Thus, he was certain that he was preparing for the escape he had announced in such an arrogant manner.

The situation was becoming intolerable. In agreement with the investigating judge, the head of the Sûreté, Mr. Dudouis, personally went to La Santé to discuss the measures that needed to be taken with the prison director. As soon as he arrived, he sent two of his men to the inmate's cell.

They lifted each of the floor tiles, disassembled the bed, did everything that is typically done in such cases, and ultimately found nothing. They were about to give up their search when the guard hurried in and said to them:

—The drawer… look at the drawer of the table. When I entered, it seemed to me that he pushed it away.

They looked, and Godzy exclaimed:

—For God's sake, this time we've got him, the culprit.

Folenfant stopped him.

—Hold on, my little friend, the chief will take inventory.

—But, this luxury cigar…

—Leave the Havana, and let's inform the chief.

Two minutes later, Mr. Dudouis was examining the drawer. He first found a bundle of newspaper clippings from the Argus de la Presse concerning Arsène Lupin, followed by a tobacco pouch, a pipe, some paper known as onion skin, and finally two books.

He glanced at the titles. One was Carlyle's *On Heroes*, an English edition, and the other was a charming Elzevir edition, bound in the period style, *The Manual of Epictetus*, a German translation published in Leiden in 1634. After flipping through them, he noticed that all the pages were scarred, underlined, and annotated. Were these conventional signs, or marks that indicated a deep affection for a book?

—We will look into this in detail, said Mr. Dudouis.

He explored the tobacco pouch and the pipe. Then, grabbing the famous gold-banded cigar, he exclaimed:

— Goodness, our friend is living well, a Henri Clet!

With a habitual gesture of a smoker, he brought it close to his ear and cracked it. Immediately, an exclamation slipped from his lips. The cigar had softened under the pressure of his fingers. He examined it more closely and soon distinguished something white between the tobacco leaves. Carefully, using a pin, he pulled out a very thin roll of paper, hardly thicker than a toothpick. It was a note. He unrolled it and read these words, written in small handwriting, likely feminine:

"The basket has taken the place of the other. Eight out of ten are prepared. By pressing with the outer foot, the panel lifts up and down. From twelve to four every day, H-P will wait. But where? Immediate response. Rest assured, your friend is watching over you."

Mr. Dudouis thought for a moment and said:

— It's quite clear... the basket... the eight compartments... From twelve to four, meaning from noon to four o'clock...

— But who is this H-P that will be waiting?

— H-P in this case must mean horsepower, right? Isn't that how we refer to the power of an engine in sports language? A twenty-four H-P refers to a car with twenty-four horsepower.

He stood up and asked:

— Is the inmate finishing lunch?

—Yes.

— And since he hasn't read this message yet, as evidenced by the state of the cigar, it's likely he just received it.

—How?

— In his food, hidden in his bread or a potato, who knows?

— Impossible, he was only allowed to have his food brought in to trap him, and we found nothing.

"We will seek Lupin's response tonight. For now, keep him away from his cell. I will take this to the examining magistrate. If he agrees with me, we will have the letter photographed immediately, and in an hour you can return to the drawer, along with these items, a cigar identical to the one that contains the original message. The prisoner must suspect nothing.

Mr. Dudouis returned that evening to the Santé prison registry with Inspector Dieuzy, a certain curiosity in his demeanor. In a corner, on the stove, three plates lay out.

—He ate?

—Yes, replied the director.

—Dieuzy, please cut these few strands of macaroni into very thin pieces and open that bread roll... Nothing?

—No, chief.

Mr. Dudouis examined the plates, the fork, the spoon, and finally the knife, a standard knife with a rounded blade. He twisted the handle to the left, then to the right. To the right, the handle gave way and unscrewed. The knife was hollow and served as a case for a sheet of paper.

—Phew! he said, it's not very clever for a man like Arsène. But let's not waste time. You, Dieuzy, go investigate that restaurant.

Then he read:

"I trust you, H-P will follow from a distance, every day. I will go ahead. See you soon, dear and admirable friend."

—Finally, exclaimed Mr. Dudouis, rubbing his hands together, I believe the matter is on the right track. A little nudge from us, and the escape will succeed... at least enough to allow us to catch the accomplices.

—And what if Arsène Lupin slips through your fingers? the director objected.

—We will employ the necessary number of men. However, if he shows too much skill... well, that's his problem! As for the gang, since the leader refuses to speak, the others will.

* * *

And indeed, Arsène Lupin didn't speak much. For months, Mr. Jules Bouvier, the investigating judge, had been trying in vain. The interrogations were reduced to uninteresting conversations between the judge and lawyer Master Danval, one of the top attorneys, who, by the way, knew about the accused as much as any random person.

From time to time, out of politeness, Arsène Lupin would drop:

—But yes, Mr. Judge, we agree: the theft at the Crédit Lyonnais, the theft on Rue de Babylone, the issuance of counterfeit banknotes, the insurance fraud, the burglaries at the châteaux of Armesnil, Gouret, Imblevain, Groseillers, and Malaquis—all of this is my doing.

—Then, could you explain to me…

—No need, I confess everything outright, everything and even ten times more than you suspect.

Out of weariness, the judge had suspended these tedious interrogations. After reviewing the two intercepted notes, he took them back. And, regularly at noon, Arsène Lupin was brought from La Santé to the Dépôt in a prison van, along with a number of other inmates. They would leave around three or four o'clock.

One afternoon, however, this return took place under particular conditions. The other inmates from La Santé had not yet been questioned, so it was decided to take Arsène Lupin back first. He therefore boarded the van alone.

These prison vans, commonly referred to as "salad baskets," are divided lengthwise by a central aisle with ten compartments opening off it—five on the right and five on the left. Each of these compartments is designed for the occupants to sit, meaning that the five prisoners are seated one above the other, while being separated by parallel partitions. A municipal guard, stationed at one end, monitors the aisle.

Arsène was placed in the third cell on the right, and the heavy van jolted to life. He realized they were leaving the Quai de l'Horloge and passing the Palais de Justice. Then, as they reached the middle of the Pont Saint-Michel, he pressed with his outer foot—that is, his right foot—against the metal plate sealing his cell, just as he did every time. Immediately, something triggered, and the metal plate gradually slid open. He could see that he was positioned right between the two wheels.

He waited, alert. The van crawled up Boulevard Saint-Michel. At the Saint-Germain intersection, it came to a halt. A horse from a truck had collapsed. With traffic halted, soon there was a congestion of carriages and omnibuses.

Arsène Lupin peered out. Another prison van was parked alongside the one he occupied. He lifted the metal plate further, placed his foot on one of the spokes of the large wheel, and jumped to the ground.

A coachman spotted him, burst out laughing, and then tried to call out. But his voice was lost in the din of the vehicles that were now moving again. Besides, Arsène Lupin was already far away.

He had taken a few steps running; but on the left sidewalk, he turned around, cast a circular glance, seemed to catch the wind, like someone who is still unsure of which direction to take. Then, resolute, he put his hands in his pockets and with the carefree air of a leisurely walker, he continued up the boulevard.

The weather was mild, a happy and light autumn day. The cafés were full. He sat at the terrace of one of them.

He ordered a beer and a pack of cigarettes. He sipped his drink slowly, smoked a cigarette calmly, and lit a second one. Finally, getting up, he asked the waiter to bring the manager.

The manager came, and Arsène said to him, loud enough to be heard by everyone:

—I'm sorry, sir, but I forgot my wallet. Perhaps my name is familiar enough for you to grant me a few days' credit: Arsène Lupin.

The manager looked at him, thinking it was a joke. But Arsène repeated:

—Lupin, inmate at La Santé, currently in a state of escape. I trust that this name inspires you with complete confidence.

And he walked away amidst laughter, without the other thinking to demand payment.

He crossed Soufflot Street diagonally and took Saint-Jacques Street. He followed it peacefully, stopping at shop windows and smoking cigarettes. On Boulevard de Port-Royal, he oriented himself, asked for directions, and walked straight towards Rue de la Santé. Soon, the grim high walls of the prison loomed. Having walked alongside them, he arrived near the municipal guard on duty, and removing his hat, he said:

—Is this indeed the prison of La Santé?

—Yes.

—I would like to return to my cell. The car left me on the way, and I wouldn't want to impose…

The guard grumbled:

—Hey there, sir, move along, and make it quick.

—Excuse me, excuse me, but my path goes through that door. And if you prevent Arsène Lupin from passing through, it could cost you dearly, my friend.

—Arsène Lupin! What are you talking about!

—I regret not having my card, said Arsène, pretending to search his pockets.

The guard looked him up and down, stunned. Then, without a word, as if compelled, he pulled a bell. The iron door creaked open.

A few minutes later, the director rushed to the office, gesticulating and feigning intense anger. Arsène smiled:

—Come now, Mr. Director, don't try to outsmart me. What is this? You take precautions to bring me back alone in the carriage, you set up a nice little trap, and you think I'm going to run away to join my friends? Well, what about the twenty security agents escorting us on foot, in a carriage, and on bicycles? No, that would have been a setup! I wouldn't have made it out alive. Tell me, Mr. Director, was that the plan?

He shrugged and added:

—I assure you, Mr. Director, that no one needs to concern themselves with me. The day I want to escape, I won't need anyone's help.

The day after, L'Écho de France, which was certainly becoming the official monitor of Arsène Lupin's exploits—rumor had it that it was one of his main sponsors—published the most comprehensive details about this escape attempt. The actual text of the notes exchanged between the inmate and his mysterious friend, the methods used for this correspondence, the complicity of the police, the stroll along Boulevard Saint-Michel, the incident at Café Soufflot —everything was revealed. It was known that Inspector Dieuzy's inquiries with the restaurant staff had yielded no results. Additionally, an astonishing fact was uncovered, showcasing the infinite variety of resources at this man's disposal: the prison van in which he had been transported was entirely rigged, having been swapped out by his gang for one of the six usual vans that make up the prison service.

The imminent escape of Arsène Lupin was no longer in doubt for anyone. He himself announced it in categorical terms, as evidenced by his response to Mr. Bouvier the day after the incident. Mocking his failure, the judge looked at him and coldly said:

—Listen closely, sir, and take my word for it: this escape attempt was part of my escape plan.

—I don't understand, the judge scoffed.

—It's unnecessary for you to understand.

And as the judge, throughout this interrogation which was published in the columns of L'Écho de France, returned to his investigation, he exclaimed wearily:

—My God, my God, what's the point! All these questions are meaningless!

—What do you mean, meaningless?

—Well, since I won't be attending my trial.

—You won't be attending…

—No, it's a fixed idea, an irrevocable decision. Nothing will make me compromise.

Such certainty, along with the inexplicable indiscretions that occurred every day, annoyed and perplexed the justice system. There were secrets that Arsène Lupin alone knew, and thus their disclosure could only come from him. But for what purpose was he revealing them? And how?

Arsène Lupin was moved to another cell. One evening, he went down to the lower floor. Meanwhile, the judge concluded his investigation and referred the case to the court of indictments.

There was silence. It lasted for two months. Arsène spent this time lying on his bed, his face almost always turned towards the wall. This change of cell seemed to have worn him down. He refused to see his lawyer and hardly exchanged a few words with his guards.

In the fortnight leading up to his trial, he appeared to revive. He complained about the lack of fresh air. They took him out to the yard in the early morning, accompanied by two men.

Public curiosity, however, had not diminished. Every day, news of his escape was anticipated. People almost wished for it, so much did they enjoy his character with his wit, cheerfulness, diversity, inventive genius, and the mystery of his life. Arsène Lupin was destined to escape. It was inevitable, fated. They even wondered why it was taking so long. Every morning, the Police Prefect would ask his secretary:

—Well, hasn't he left yet?

—No, Mr. Prefect.

—Then it will be tomorrow.

On the eve of the trial, a man showed up at the offices of the Grand Journal, asked for the legal collaborator, threw his business card in his face, and quickly walked away. The card bore the words: "Arsène Lupin always keeps his promises."

* * *

It was under these circumstances that the proceedings began.

The turnout was massive. Everyone wanted to see the famous Arsène Lupin and savor the way he would outsmart the president. Lawyers and judges, journalists and socialites, artists and women of society—all of Paris crowded into the courtroom.

It was raining, and outside the day was dark; Arsène Lupin was hardly visible when the guards brought him in. However, his heavy demeanor, the way he dropped into his seat, and his indifferent, passive stillness did not work in his favor. Several times, his lawyer—one of Me Danval's secretaries, who found the role he was reduced to unworthy of him—addressed him. He nodded his head and remained silent.

The clerk read the charges, then the president stated:

—Accused, please stand. Your name, first name, age, and profession?

Receiving no response, he repeated:

—Your name? I am asking for your name?

A thick, tired voice articulated:

—Baudru, Désiré.

There were murmurs in the courtroom. But the president continued:

—Baudru, Désiré? Ah! Well, a new alias! Since this is about the eighth name you claim, and it is likely as imaginary as the others, we will stick, if you don't mind, to the name Arsène Lupin, under which you are more favorably known.

The president consulted his notes and continued:

—Sir, despite all the investigations, it has been impossible to reconstruct your identity. You present a rather unique case in our modern society of having no past. We do not know who you are, where you come from, where your childhood was spent—essentially, nothing. You suddenly appeared three years ago, and we do not know exactly from what background, to reveal yourself as Arsène Lupin, which means a strange blend of intelligence and perversion, immorality and generosity. The information we have about you prior to that time is mainly speculation. It is likely that a certain Rostat, who worked eight years ago alongside the magician Dickson, was none other than Arsène Lupin. It is probable that the Russian student who attended Dr. Altier's laboratory at the Saint-Louis hospital six years ago, who often surprised his mentor with the ingenuity of his hypotheses on bacteriology and the boldness of his experiments in skin diseases, was Arsène Lupin as well. Arsène Lupin, we believe, is also the Japanese wrestling instructor who established himself in Paris long before jiu-jitsu was even mentioned there. Arsène Lupin might also be the cyclist who won the Grand Prix at the Exhibition, collected his 10,000 francs, and then vanished. Perhaps Arsène Lupin is also the one who saved so many people through the small window of the Bazar de la Charité... and then robbed them.

And, after a pause, the president concluded:

—Such is this period, which seems to have been nothing but a meticulous preparation for the struggle you have undertaken against society, a methodical training where you honed your strength, energy, and skill to the highest degree. Do you acknowledge the accuracy of these facts?

During this speech, the accused swayed from one leg to the other, his back hunched, his arms limp. Under the brighter light, his extreme thinness was noticeable, his hollow cheeks, his strangely prominent cheekbones, his earth-colored face marbled with small red patches, and framed by an uneven and sparse beard. Prison had aged and withered him considerably. The elegant silhouette and youthful face that newspapers had often published in sympathetic portraits were no longer recognizable.

It seemed he had not heard the question that was posed to him. It was repeated to him twice. Then he lifted his eyes, appeared to think for a moment, and then, making a violent effort, murmured:

—Baudru, Désiré.

The president began to laugh.

—I don't quite understand the defense strategy you've adopted, Arsène Lupin. If it's to play the fool and act as though you're irresponsible, that's up to you. As for me, I will get straight to the point without worrying about your whims.

And he went into detail about the thefts, scams, and forgeries attributed to Lupin. Occasionally, he questioned the accused. Lupin would grunt or fail to respond.

The parade of witnesses began. There were several insignificant testimonies, and others more serious, all sharing the common trait of contradicting one another. A troubling obscurity enveloped the proceedings, but then Chief Inspector Ganimard was brought in, and interest was rekindled.

From the very beginning, however, the old policeman caused a certain disappointment. He did not seem intimidated—he had seen much worse—but rather worried, uncomfortable. Several times, he cast a visibly uneasy glance at the accused. Nevertheless, with both hands resting on the stand, he recounted the incidents he had been involved in, his pursuit across Europe, his arrival in America. And he was listened to with eagerness, as one would listen to the tale of the most thrilling adventures. But towards the end, having alluded to his conversations with Arsène Lupin, he stopped twice, distracted and unsure.

It was clear that another thought was occupying his mind. The president said to him:

—If you are unwell, it would be better to interrupt your testimony.

—No, no, it's just…

He fell silent, looked at the accused for a long time, deeply, then said:

—I request permission to examine the accused more closely. There is a mystery here that I must clarify.

He approached, observed him even more intently, his full attention focused, then returned to the stand. And there, in a somewhat solemn tone, he declared:

—Mr. President, I assert that the man who is here, in front of me, is not Arsène Lupin.

A great silence greeted these words. The president, initially taken aback, exclaimed:

—What! What are you saying? You must be crazy.

The inspector calmly asserted:

—At first glance, one might be misled by a resemblance, which indeed exists, I admit, but it only takes a second of attention. The nose, the mouth, the hair, the skin color... in short: this is not Arsène Lupin. And the eyes! Has he ever had those alcoholic eyes?

—Come now, let's clarify this. What are you claiming, witness?

"—Do I know! He must have replaced a poor soul who was about to be condemned in his place... Unless it's a partner in crime.

Cries, laughter, and exclamations erupted from all sides in the room, stirred by this unexpected turn of events. The president called for the investigating judge, the director of the health facility, and the guards, and suspended the hearing.

When it resumed, Mr. Bouvier and the director, face-to-face with the accused, stated that there was only a very vague resemblance between Arsène Lupin and this man.

—But then, exclaimed the president, who is this man? Where does he come from? How did he end up in the hands of justice?

The two guards from the health facility were brought in. In a stunning contradiction, they recognized the inmate they had been watching in turn! The president breathed a sigh of relief.

But one of the guards added:

—Yes, yes, I believe it is him.

—What do you mean, you believe?

—Well, I've barely seen him. He was delivered to me in the evening, and for the past two months, he has always been lying against the wall.

—But before these two months?

—Ah! Before, he did not occupy cell 24.

The director of the prison clarified this point:

—We changed the inmate's cell after his escape attempt.

—But you, Mr. Director, you have seen him in the last two months?

—I haven't had the chance to see him... he kept to himself.

—And this man is not the inmate who was handed over to you?

—No.

—Then who is he?

—I couldn't say.

—So we are faced with a substitution that must have taken place two months ago. How do you explain that?

—It's impossible.

—So?

In despair, the president turned to the accused and, in an inviting voice:"

"Well, accused, could you explain how and since when you have been in the hands of justice?"

It seemed that this benevolent tone disarmed the man's suspicion or stimulated his understanding. He tried to respond. Finally, skillfully and gently questioned, he managed to gather a few sentences, from which it emerged that two months earlier, he had been brought to the Dépôt. He had spent one night and one morning there. Possessing a sum of seventy-five cents, he had been released. However, as he was crossing the courtyard, two guards took him by the arm and led him to the prison van. Since then, he had been living in cell 24, not unhappy... the food was good... the sleep was decent... Therefore, he had not protested...

All of this seemed plausible. Amid laughter and great excitement, the president referred the case to another session for further investigation.

* * *

The investigation immediately established this fact recorded in the register: eight weeks prior, a man named Baudru Désiré had stayed at the Dépôt. Released the next day, he left the Dépôt at two in the afternoon. Now, on that day, at two o'clock, questioned for the last time, Arsène Lupin was coming out of the investigation and departing in a prison van.

Had the guards made a mistake? Misled by the resemblance, had they, in a moment of inattention, substituted this man for their prisoner? It would really require a level of complacency that their service records did not allow one to assume.

Was the substitution planned in advance? Aside from the fact that the layout of the place made it almost unfeasible, it would have required Baudru to be an accomplice and to have allowed himself to be arrested with the specific aim of taking Arsène Lupin's place. But then, by what miracle could such a plan, solely based on a series of unlikely chances, random encounters, and fantastical errors, have succeeded?

Désiré Baudru was taken to the anthropometric service: there were no records matching his description. Moreover, his traces were easily found. In Courbevoie, Asnières, and Levallois, he was known. He lived off charity and slept in one of those shanties where ragpickers crowd near the Ternes barrier. However, he had disappeared for the past year.

Had he been recruited by Arsène Lupin? Nothing suggested that this was true. And even if it were, we still would not know more about the prisoner's escape. The mystery remained the same. Of the twenty hypotheses trying to explain it, none were satisfactory. The escape itself was beyond doubt, and it was an escape that was incomprehensible and impressive, where the public, as well as justice, sensed the effort of long preparation, a series of actions wonderfully intertwined, culminating in a conclusion that justified Arsène Lupin's proud prediction: "I will not attend my trial."

After a month of meticulous investigation, the mystery remained just as indecipherable. However, they could not keep poor Baudru indefinitely. His trial would have been ridiculous: what charges did they have against him? His release was signed by the examining magistrate. But the head of the Security Service decided to establish active surveillance around him.

The idea came from Ganimard. From his perspective, there was neither complicity nor coincidence. Baudru was merely a tool that Arsène Lupin had skillfully manipulated. With Baudru free, they could trace back to Arsène Lupin or at least to someone in his gang.

Ganimard was joined by the two inspectors Folenfant and Dieuzy, and one January morning, on a foggy day, the prison gates opened for Baudru Désiré.

He initially appeared quite confused, walking like a man who has no clear idea of how to spend his time. He followed the Rue de la Santé and the Rue Saint-Jacques. In front of a second-hand shop, he took off his jacket and vest, sold his vest for a few coins, and, putting his jacket back on, walked away.

He crossed the Seine. At Châtelet, an omnibus passed him by. He wanted to get on, but there was no room. The conductor advised him to take a number, so he entered the waiting room.

At that moment, Ganimard called his two men over and, without taking his eyes off the office, he said hurriedly:

"Get a cab... no, two, that's safer. I'll go with one of you, and we'll follow him."

The men obeyed. Meanwhile, Baudru did not appear. Ganimard stepped forward: there was no one in the waiting room.

"What an idiot I am," he murmured, "I forgot about the second exit."

The office indeed communicates through an interior corridor with that of the Rue Saint-Martin. Ganimard rushed forward. He arrived just in time to see Baudru on the upper deck of the Batignolles-Jardin des Plantes bus turning the corner onto the Rue de Rivoli. He ran and caught up with the omnibus. But he had lost his two agents. He was alone in continuing the chase.

In his fury, he was about to grab him by the collar without further ado. Wasn't it with premeditation and clever trickery that this so-called fool had separated him from his aides?

He looked at Baudru. He was dozing on the bench, his head bobbing from side to side. With his mouth slightly open, his face bore an incredible expression of stupidity. No, this was not an opponent capable of outsmarting the old Ganimard. It was pure chance that had helped him, that was all.

At the Galeries-Lafayette intersection, the man jumped from the omnibus onto the Muette tram. They followed Boulevard Haussmann, then Avenue Victor-Hugo. Baudru only got off in front of the Muette station. And with a nonchalant step, he plunged into the Bois de Boulogne.

He moved from one path to another, retraced his steps, and wandered away. What was he looking for? Did he have a purpose?

After an hour of this behavior, he appeared exhausted. In fact, spotting a bench, he sat down. The place, located not far from Auteuil, by the edge of a small lake hidden among the trees, was completely deserted. Half an hour passed. Growing impatient, Ganimard decided to start a conversation.

He approached and took a seat next to Baudru. He lit a cigarette, drew circles in the sand with the tip of his cane, and said:

—It's not hot out.

A silence. And suddenly, within that silence, a burst of laughter echoed—joyful laughter, the kind of laughter from a child caught in a fit of giggles, unable to stop. Ganimard distinctly felt his hair stand on end at the exposed skin of his scalp. That laughter, that infernal laughter he knew so well!...

With a sudden movement, he grabbed the man by the lapels of his jacket and looked deeply, violently into his eyes—more intensely than he had during the trial. And in truth, he no longer saw just the man. He saw the man, but at the same time, he saw the other, the real one.

Guided by a conspiratorial will, he rediscovered the fiery life in those eyes, he completed the emaciated mask, he glimpsed the real flesh beneath the ravaged skin, the true mouth behind the grimace that distorted it. And those were the eyes of the other, the mouth of the other, but above all, it was his sharp, lively, mocking, witty expression—so clear and so youthful!

—Arsène Lupin, Arsène Lupin, he stammered.

And suddenly, filled with rage, tightening his grip around his throat, he tried to throw him off balance. Despite being fifty years old, he still possessed remarkable strength, while his opponent seemed to be in rather poor condition. And what a masterstroke it would be if he could capture him!

The struggle was brief. Arsène Lupin hardly defended himself, and just as quickly as he had attacked, Ganimard released his grip. His right arm hung limp, numb.

—If they taught you jiu-jitsu at the Quai des Orfèvres, Lupin declared, you would know that this move is called udi-shi-ghi in Japanese.

And he added coldly:

—One more second, and I would have broken your arm, and you would have only received what you deserve. How could you, an old friend whom I respect, to whom I reveal my true self without hesitation, abuse my trust! That's wrong... So, what is it?

Ganimard remained silent. This escape, for which he felt responsible —wasn't it him who, through his sensational testimony, had misled the justice system?—this escape seemed to him the shame of his career. A tear rolled down toward his gray mustache.

—Oh my God, Ganimard, don't get worked up: if you hadn't spoken, I would have made sure someone else would. Come on, could I accept that Baudru Désiré be condemned?

—So, murmured Ganimard, it was you who were over there? It's you who are here!

—Me, always me, only me.

—Is that possible?

—Oh! There's no need to be a sorcerer. It just takes, as that good president said, about twelve years of preparation to be ready for any eventuality.

—But your face? Your eyes?

—You understand well that if I worked for eighteen months in Saint-Louis with Doctor Altier, it wasn't out of love for the art. I thought that anyone who would one day have the honor of calling themselves Arsène Lupin must rise above the ordinary laws of appearance and identity. Appearance? But it can be altered at will. A certain hypodermic injection of paraffin can swell your skin just at the chosen spot. Pyrogallol can transform you into a Mohican. The sap of greater celandine can adorn you with skin lesions and tumors that have the most pleasing effect. One chemical method affects the growth of your beard and hair, while another alters the sound of your voice. Combine this with two months of dieting in cell number 24, along with countless exercises to open my mouth in just the right grimace, to tilt my head at this angle, and to curve my back in this way. Finally, five drops of atropine in the eyes to make them wild and evasive, and the transformation is complete.

— I don't understand how the guards…

—The metamorphosis was gradual. They couldn't notice the daily evolution.

—But Baudru Désiré?

—Baudru exists. He is a poor innocent whom I met last year, and he truly does share certain similarities with me. Anticipating a possible arrest, I took steps to ensure his safety, and I focused on identifying the differences between us from the start, in order to minimize them as much as possible. My friends arranged for him to spend a night in the local jail, so that he would be released around the same time as I was, making the coincidence easy to establish. Because, mark my words, it was necessary to trace his movements; otherwise, the authorities would have questioned who I was. By presenting this excellent Baudru, it was inevitable, you understand, inevitable that they would latch onto him, and despite the insurmountable challenges of a substitution, they would prefer to believe in the substitution rather than admit their ignorance.

—Yes, yes, indeed, murmured Ganimard.

—And then, exclaimed Arsène Lupin, I had a tremendous advantage, a card I had crafted from the very beginning: the expectation that everyone had of my escape. And that is indeed the gross mistake you and the others made in this thrilling game that justice and I were engaged in, with my freedom as the stake: you presumed once again that I was acting out of bravado, that I was intoxicated by my successes like a naïve fool. Me, Arsène Lupin, such a weakness! And just as in the Cahorn affair, you did not consider: "Since Arsène Lupin is proclaiming from the rooftops that he will escape, it means he has reasons that compel him to do so." But, goodness, understand that in order to escape… without actually escaping, it was essential for everyone to believe in that escape in advance, that it was a matter of faith, an absolute conviction, a truth as bright as the sun. And that was my intention. Arsène Lupin would escape; Arsène Lupin would not attend his trial. And when you stood up to say, "this man is not Arsène Lupin," it would have been supernatural for everyone not to immediately believe that I was not Arsène Lupin. If just one person had doubted, if just one had expressed this simple reservation: "What if it is Arsène Lupin?" at that very moment, I would have been lost. It was enough to lean toward me, not with the notion that I wasn't Arsène Lupin, as you and the others did, but with the idea that I could be Arsène Lupin, and despite all my precautions, I would be recognized. But I was calm. Logically, psychologically, no one could have that simple little idea.

He suddenly grasped Ganimard's hand.

—Come now, Ganimard, admit that eight days after our meeting in the Santé prison, you waited for me at four o'clock at your home, just as I asked?

—And your prison transport? Ganimard replied, avoiding the question.

—Just a ruse! My friends patched up and substituted that old, out-of-service vehicle, hoping to give it a shot. But I knew it was impractical without exceptional circumstances. However, I found it useful to carry out this escape attempt and give it as much publicity as possible. A first escape, boldly planned, would lend the second the credibility of a prearranged escape.

—So the cigar…

—Hollowed out by me, just like the knife.

—And the banknotes?

—Written by me.

—And the mysterious correspondent?

—She and I are one and the same. I can write in her style at will.

Ganimard paused for a moment and countered:

—How is it possible that in the anthropometry department, when they took Baudru's file, they didn't notice it matched Arsène Lupin's?

—The file for Arsène Lupin doesn't exist.

—Come now!

—Or at least it's false. It's a question I've studied extensively. The Bertillon system first relies on visual identification—and you can see that it's not infallible—and then on measurements: head, fingers, ears, etc. In that regard, there's nothing to be done.

—So?

—So, I had to pay. Even before my return from America, one of the employees in the service was willing to record a false measure at the start of my measurements. This is enough for the entire system to go off track, causing a file to point to a location that is diametrically opposed to where it should end up. Therefore, the Baudru file should not coincide with the Arsène Lupin file.

There was another silence, then Ganimard asked:

—And now, what will you do?

—Now, exclaimed Lupin, I will rest, follow a regimen of overindulgence, and gradually become myself again. It's fine to be Baudru or someone else, to change personalities as easily as changing shirts and to choose one's appearance, voice, gaze, and handwriting. But there are times when you can lose yourself in all of that, and it's quite sad. Right now, I feel like the man who lost his shadow. I will search for myself... and find myself again.

He walked back and forth. A bit of darkness mingled with the daylight. He stopped in front of Ganimard.

—I believe we have nothing more to say to each other?

—Yes, replied the inspector, I would like to know if you will reveal the truth about your escape... The mistake I made...

—Oh! no one will ever know that it was Arsène Lupin who was released. I have too much interest in surrounding myself with the most mysterious shadows to not let this escape retain its almost miraculous quality. So, do not worry, my good friend, and goodbye. I'm dining in town tonight, and I only have time to dress.

—I thought you were so eager for rest!

—Alas! there are social obligations from which one cannot escape. The rest will begin tomorrow.

—And where are you dining?

—At the British Embassy.

CHAPTER FOUR
THE MYSTERIOUS TRAVELER

The day before, I had sent my car to Rouen by road. I was supposed to join it there by train, and from there, go to visit some friends who live by the Seine.

Now, in Paris, just a few minutes before departure, seven gentlemen invaded my compartment; five of them were smoking. No matter how short the journey would be, the thought of taking it in such company was unpleasant, especially since the old-fashioned carriage had no corridor. So I took my overcoat, my newspapers, my timetable, and sought refuge in one of the adjoining compartments.

A lady was already there. Upon seeing me, she made a gesture of annoyance that did not escape me, and she leaned towards a man standing on the footboard, her husband, no doubt, who had accompanied her to the station. The man observed me, and his assessment likely ended in my favor, as he spoke softly to his wife, smiling, with the kind of reassurance one offers a frightened child. She smiled back and gave me a friendly glance, as if she suddenly understood that I was one of those gallant men with whom a woman can remain locked up for two hours in a small six-foot square box without having anything to fear.

Her husband said to her:

—You won't hold it against me, my dear, but I have an urgent appointment, and I can't wait.

He affectionately kissed her and left. She sent him discreet little kisses through the window and waved her handkerchief.

But a whistle blew. The train began to move.

At that precise moment, and despite the protests of the staff, the door swung open, and a man burst into our compartment. My companion, who was standing at the time and organizing her belongings along the netting, let out a cry of terror and fell onto the seat.

I am not a coward, far from it, but I admit that these last-minute interruptions are always distressing. They seem ambiguous, unnatural. There must be something behind it, otherwise...

However, the appearance of the newcomer and his demeanor would have softened the negative impression created by his actions. There was a certain decorum, almost elegance, a tasteful tie, clean gloves, an energetic face... But, where on earth had I seen that face before? There was no doubt about it; I had seen it. More precisely, I was recalling the kind of memory that lingers after seeing a portrait several times without ever having seen the original. At the same time, I felt the futility of any effort to remember, as that memory was so insubstantial and vague.

But, refocusing my attention on the lady, I was astonished by her pallor and the turmoil in her features. She was looking at her neighbor—they were sitting on the same side—with an expression of genuine terror, and I noticed that one of her trembling hands was sliding toward a small travel bag placed on the seat about twenty centimeters from her knees. She eventually grasped it and pulled it nervously against her.

Our eyes met, and I could read so much discomfort and anxiety in hers that I couldn't help but say to her:

—You're not unwell, Madam? Should I open this window?

Without answering me, she pointed fearfully at the individual. I smiled as her husband had done, shrugged, and indicated with gestures that she had nothing to fear, that I was there, and besides, that this gentleman seemed quite harmless.

At that moment, he turned to us, looking each of us up and down, then retreated into his corner and remained still.

There was silence, but the lady, as if she had gathered all her energy to perform a desperate act, said to me in a barely intelligible voice:

—Do you know he is on our train?

—Who?

—But him… him… I assure you.

—Who, him?

—Arsène Lupin!

She had not taken her eyes off the traveler, and it was to him rather than to me that she threw the syllables of that alarming name.

He lowered his hat over his eyes. Was it to hide his agitation or was he simply preparing to sleep?

I raised this objection:

—Arsène Lupin was sentenced yesterday, in absentia, to twenty years of hard labor. It seems unlikely that he would take the risk of showing himself in public today. Moreover, didn't the newspapers report his presence in Turkey this winter, following his famous escape from La Santé?

—He is on this train, the lady repeated, with an increasingly marked intention to be heard by our companion. My husband is deputy director of penitentiary services, and it was the station commissioner himself who told us they were looking for Arsène Lupin.

—That's not a reason…

—He was seen in the waiting room. He bought a first-class ticket to Rouen.

—It would have been easy to catch him.

—He vanished. The conductor at the entrance to the waiting rooms did not see him, but it was assumed he had gone through the suburban platforms and boarded the express that leaves ten minutes after us.

—In that case, he would have been caught.

—And if, at the last moment, he jumped off that express to come here, on our train… as is likely… as is certain?

—In that case, this is where he will be caught. For the employees and agents will surely have noticed this transfer from one train to another, and when we arrive in Rouen, he will be picked up quite neatly.

—Him? Never! He will find a way to escape again.

—In that case, I wish him a good trip.

—But until then, all he can do!

—What?

—Do I know? We must expect anything!

She was very agitated, and indeed the situation justified this nervous excitement to a certain extent. Almost despite myself, I said to her:

—There are indeed some curious coincidences... But calm down. Assuming that Arsène Lupin is in one of those cars, he will behave himself, and rather than attract new troubles, he will have no other idea than to avoid the danger that threatens him.

My words did not reassure her at all. However, she fell silent, perhaps fearing to be indiscreet.

I spread out my newspapers and read the reports on the trial of Arsène Lupin. Since they contained nothing new, they held only moderate interest for me. Furthermore, I was tired, having slept poorly, and I felt my eyelids grow heavy and my head tilt.

—But, sir, you're not going to sleep!

The lady snatched my newspapers away and looked at me with indignation.

—Of course not, I replied, I have no desire to do so.

—That would be extremely imprudent, she said to me.

—Extremely, I echoed.

And I fought vigorously, clinging to the landscape, to the clouds streaking the sky. Soon, everything blurred in space, the image of the agitated lady and the dozing man faded from my mind, and within me, there was the great, profound silence of sleep.

Inconsistent and light dreams soon adorned my mind, and a being who played the role and bore the name Arsène Lupin held a certain place within them. He moved on the horizon, his back laden with precious items, passing through walls and emptying castles.

But the silhouette of this being, who was no longer Arsène Lupin, became clearer. He approached me, growing larger, leaped into the train car with incredible agility, and landed squarely on my chest.

A sharp pain… a piercing scream… I woke up. The man, the traveler, with one knee on my chest, was gripping my throat.

I saw this very vaguely, as my eyes were bloodshot. I also noticed the lady convulsing in a corner, experiencing a nervous attack. I didn't even try to resist. Besides, I wouldn't have had the strength: my temples were buzzing, I was gasping… I was choking… One more minute… and it would be asphyxiation.

The man must have sensed it. He loosened his grip. Without stepping back, with his right hand, he extended a rope where he had prepared a noose, and with a swift motion, he bound my wrists together. In an instant, I was tied up, gagged, immobilized.

And he carried out this task in the most natural way possible, with an ease that revealed the expertise of a master, a professional in theft and crime. Not a word, not a frantic movement. Just cold-bloodedness and audacity. And there I was, on the bench, tied up like a mummy, me, Arsène Lupin!

In truth, there was much to laugh about. And despite the seriousness of the circumstances, I couldn't help but appreciate all the irony and flavor in the situation. Arsène Lupin taken in like a novice! Robbed like any common person—because, of course, the bandit relieved me of my purse and wallet! Arsène Lupin, a victim this time, duped, defeated… What an adventure!

Then there was the lady. He didn't even pay her any attention. He simply picked up the small bag that lay on the carpet and extracted the jewelry, wallet, and trinkets of gold and silver that it contained. The lady opened one eye, gasped in horror, removed her rings, and held them out to the man as if she wanted to spare him any unnecessary effort. He took the rings and looked at her: she fainted.

Then, still silent and calm, without paying us any further mind, he returned to his seat, lit a cigarette, and began to thoroughly examine the treasures he had acquired, an examination that seemed to satisfy him completely.

I was much less satisfied. I'm not talking about the twelve thousand francs from which I had been unjustly stripped: that was a loss I accepted only temporarily, and I fully expected those twelve thousand francs to return to my possession very soon, along with the very important papers contained in my wallet: plans, estimates, addresses, lists of correspondents, compromising letters. But for the moment, a more immediate and serious concern was troubling me:

What was going to happen next?

As one might expect, the commotion caused by my passage through the Saint-Lazare station did not escape my notice. Invited by friends who knew me as Guillaume Berlat, and for whom my resemblance to Arsène Lupin was a source of affectionate jokes, I had not been able to disguise myself as I wished, and my presence had been noted. Furthermore, someone had seen a man, undoubtedly Arsène Lupin, rush from the express train to the local train. Therefore, inevitably, the police chief of Rouen, alerted by telegram and assisted by a respectable number of officers, would be waiting at the train's arrival to question suspicious passengers and conduct a thorough inspection of the carriages.

I anticipated all of this and was not overly concerned, confident that the Rouen police would not be any more perceptive than their Paris counterparts, and that I would manage to go unnoticed—would it not suffice for me to casually show my deputy's ID as I exited, with which I had already inspired complete trust in the Saint-Lazare conductor? But how much things had changed! I was no longer free. It was impossible to attempt one of my usual tricks. In one of the carriages, the commissioner would find Mr. Arsène Lupin, delivered to him by a fortunate coincidence, tied up and compliant as a lamb, packaged and all set. He would simply have to take delivery, just like receiving a postal package addressed to you at the station, a game bag or a basket of fruits and vegetables.

And to avoid this unfortunate outcome, what could I do, wrapped up in my bandages?

Meanwhile, the train sped towards Rouen, the only next stop, burning past Vernon and Saint-Pierre.

Another problem intrigued me, one that I was less directly involved in, but whose solution piqued my professional curiosity. What were my companion's intentions?

If I had been alone, he would have had the time, in Rouen, to descend quietly. But what about the lady? No sooner would the door be opened than she, so wise and humble at that moment, would scream, flail about, and call for help!

And that was my astonishment! Why didn't he reduce her to the same helplessness as me, which would have given him the opportunity to disappear before anyone noticed his double wrongdoing?

He continued to smoke, his eyes fixed on the space that a hesitant rain was beginning to streak with large diagonal lines. Once, however, he turned away, grabbed my indicator, and consulted it.

The lady, on her part, was trying to remain fainted to reassure her enemy. But bouts of coughing, provoked by the smoke, betrayed her fainting.

As for me, I felt quite uncomfortable and very sore. And I was thinking... I was plotting...

Pont-de-l'Arche, Oissel... The express train sped along, joyful, intoxicated by its speed.

Saint-Étienne... At that moment, the man stood up and took two steps towards us, prompting the lady to respond with a new scream and a genuinely fainting spell.

But what was his goal? He lowered the window on our side. The rain was now falling heavily, and his gesture indicated the annoyance he felt for not having an umbrella or overcoat. He glanced at the bag: the lady's snack was inside. He took it. He also took my overcoat and put it on.

We were crossing the Seine. He rolled up the bottom of his pants, then bent down and lifted the outside latch.

Would he throw himself onto the tracks? At that speed, it would have meant certain death. They rushed into the tunnel under the Sainte-Catherine hill. The man opened the door slightly and, with his foot, felt for the first step. What madness! The darkness, the smoke, the noise—everything made such a move seem fantastical. But suddenly, the train slowed down; the Westinghouse brakes resisted the wheels' effort. Within a minute, the speed became normal, then decreased further. Undoubtedly, construction work was planned in this part of the tunnel, which required the trains to slow down, perhaps for a few days now, and the man knew this.

He simply had to place his other foot on the step, descend to the second one, and leave quietly, not before having pulled the latch down and closed the door.

Barely had he disappeared when the light pierced through the whiter smoke. They emerged into a valley. One more tunnel and they would be in Rouen.

Immediately, the lady regained her composure, and her first concern was to lament the loss of her jewelry. I implored her with my eyes. She understood and freed me from the gag that was choking me. She also wanted to untie my bonds, but I stopped her.

—No, no, the police must see things as they are. I want them to be informed about this scoundrel.

—And what if I pull the alarm bell?

—Too late, you should have thought of that while he was attacking me.

—But he would have killed me! Oh! Sir, didn't I tell you he was traveling on this train? I recognized him immediately from his portrait. And now he's gone with my jewelry.

—We will find him, don't worry.

—Find Arsène Lupin! Never.

—It depends on you, Madame. Listen. As soon as we arrive, be at the door and call out, make some noise. Agents and staff will come. Then tell them what you saw, in a few words, the assault I was a victim of and Arsène Lupin's escape. Provide a description: a soft hat, an umbrella—yours—and a tailored gray overcoat.

—Yours, she said.

—What, mine? No, his. I didn't have one.

—I thought he didn't have one either when he got on.

—Yes, yes… unless it was a piece of clothing left in the net. In any case, he had it when he got off, and that's what matters… a tailored gray overcoat, remember… Oh! I forgot… state your name right away. Your husband's position will encourage everyone's eagerness.

We were arriving. She was already leaning toward the door. I raised my voice a bit, almost imperiously, so my words would stick in her mind.

—Also mention my name, Guillaume Berlat. If necessary, say that you know me… That will save us time… we need to expedite the preliminary investigation… the important thing is to pursue Arsène

Lupin... your jewelry... There's no mistake, right? Guillaume Berlat, a friend of your husband.

—Understood... Guillaume Berlat.

She was already calling out and gesturing. The train hadn't stopped when a gentleman boarded, followed by several men. The critical moment had arrived.

Breathless, the lady exclaimed:

—Arsène Lupin... he attacked us... he stole my jewelry... I am Mrs. Renaud... my husband is the deputy director of penitentiary services... Ah! Look, here is my brother, Georges Ardelle, director of Crédit Rouennais... you should know...

She kissed a young man who had just joined us, and whom the commissioner greeted, and she continued, distressed:

— Yes, Arsène Lupin... while Mr. was sleeping, he lunged for his throat... Mr. Berlat, a friend of my husband.

The commissioner asked:

— But where is he, Arsène Lupin?

— He jumped from the train under the tunnel, after the Seine.

— Are you sure it was him?

— Am I sure! I recognized him perfectly. Besides, he was seen at the Saint-Lazare station. He was wearing a soft hat...

— No, not... a hard felt hat, like this one, the commissioner corrected, pointing to my hat.

— A soft hat, I assure you, Mrs. Renaud repeated, and a gray overcoat with a fitted waist.

— Indeed, murmured the commissioner, the telegram mentions this gray overcoat, fitted with a black velvet collar.

— A black velvet collar, precisely, Mrs. Renaud exclaimed triumphantly.

I breathed a sigh of relief. Ah! what a brave, excellent friend I had!

Meanwhile, the officers had removed my restraints. I bit my lips hard, causing them to bleed. Bent over, with a handkerchief over my mouth, as one does when they've been in an uncomfortable position for a long time and bear the bloody mark of a gag on their face, I said to the commissioner, in a weakened voice:

— Sir, it was Arsène Lupin, there's no doubt about it... If you hurry, you can catch him... I believe I can be of some help to you...

The car designated for the justice's investigations was detached. The train continued towards Le Havre. We were led toward the station-master's office, through the crowd of curious onlookers crowding the platform.

At that moment, I hesitated. Under some pretext, I could slip away, find my car, and make a quick getaway. Waiting was dangerous. If anything happened, if a telegram arrived from Paris, I would be lost.

Yes, but what about my thief? Left to my own devices in an area that wasn't very familiar to me, I couldn't hope to catch up with him.

—Well! Let's take a chance, I thought, and stay. The game is hard to win, but so enjoyable to play! And the stakes are worth it.

And, as we were asked to temporarily renew our statements, I exclaimed:

—Mr. Commissioner, right now Arsène Lupin is getting ahead. My car is waiting for me in the courtyard. If you would be so kind as to come with me, we could try...

The commissioner smiled slyly:

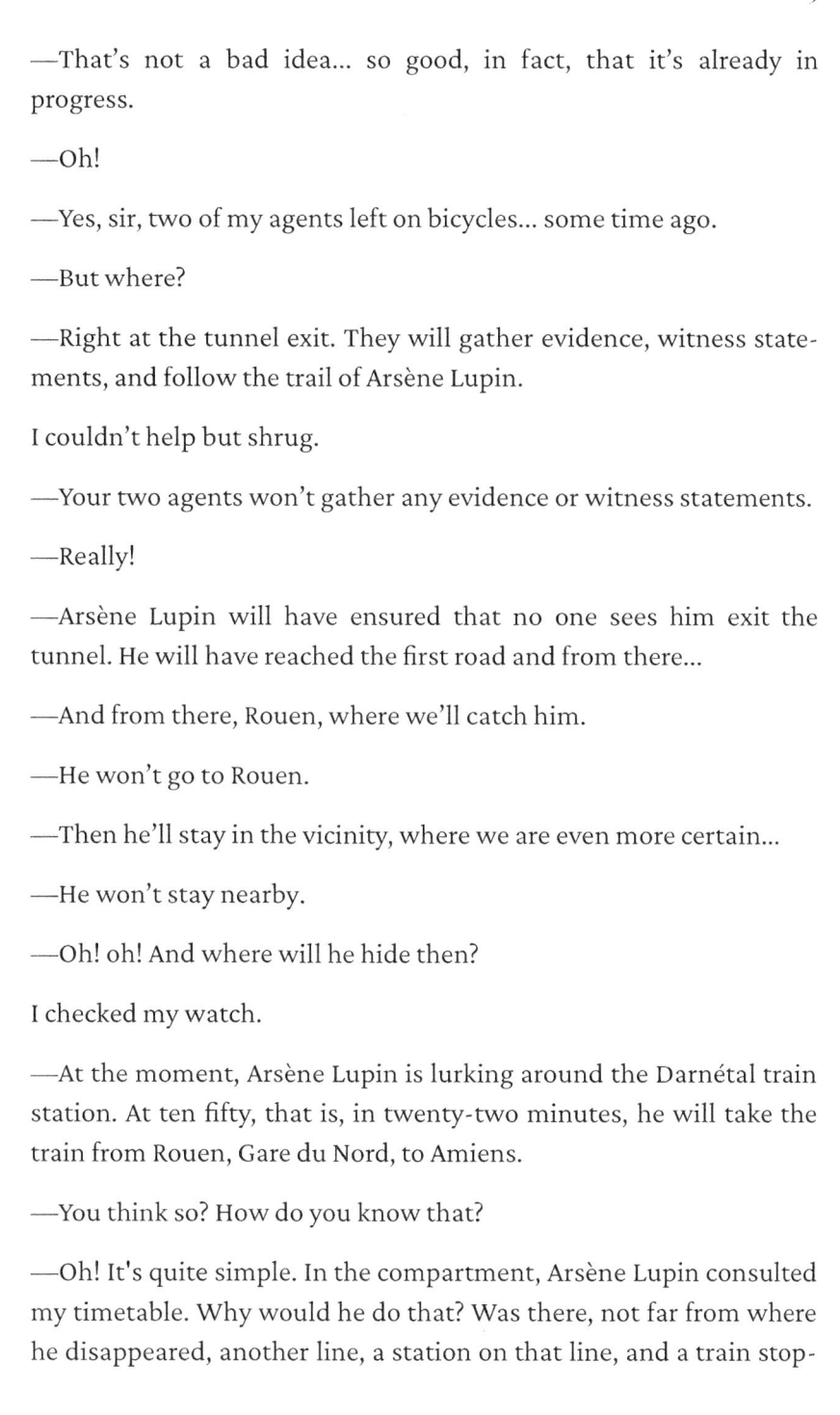

—That's not a bad idea... so good, in fact, that it's already in progress.

—Oh!

—Yes, sir, two of my agents left on bicycles... some time ago.

—But where?

—Right at the tunnel exit. They will gather evidence, witness statements, and follow the trail of Arsène Lupin.

I couldn't help but shrug.

—Your two agents won't gather any evidence or witness statements.

—Really!

—Arsène Lupin will have ensured that no one sees him exit the tunnel. He will have reached the first road and from there...

—And from there, Rouen, where we'll catch him.

—He won't go to Rouen.

—Then he'll stay in the vicinity, where we are even more certain...

—He won't stay nearby.

—Oh! oh! And where will he hide then?

I checked my watch.

—At the moment, Arsène Lupin is lurking around the Darnétal train station. At ten fifty, that is, in twenty-two minutes, he will take the train from Rouen, Gare du Nord, to Amiens.

—You think so? How do you know that?

—Oh! It's quite simple. In the compartment, Arsène Lupin consulted my timetable. Why would he do that? Was there, not far from where he disappeared, another line, a station on that line, and a train stopping at that station? I, too, have just consulted the timetable. It informed me.

—Indeed, sir, said the commissioner, that's wonderfully deduced. What skill!

Driven by my conviction, I had made a blunder by showing off so much cleverness. He looked at me in astonishment, and I sensed a flicker of suspicion crossing his mind. —Oh! barely, for the photographs sent from all directions by the prosecutor's office were too imperfect, showing a version of Arsène Lupin that was too different from the one he had in front of him, making it impossible for him to recognize me. Still, he was troubled, vaguely uneasy.

There was a moment of silence. Something ambiguous and uncertain held back our words. I myself felt a shiver of discomfort. Was fortune about to turn against me? Overcoming it, I started to laugh.

—My God, nothing sharpens your understanding like the loss of a wallet and the desire to find it. And it seems to me that if you would kindly assign two of your agents to me, we might be able to...

—Oh! Please, Commissioner, Madame Renaud exclaimed, listen to Mr. Berlat.

The intervention of my excellent friend was decisive. Pronounced by her, the wife of an influential figure, the name Berlat truly became mine and granted me an identity that no suspicion could touch. The commissioner stood up:

—I would be very happy, Mr. Berlat, believe me, to see you succeed. Just like you, I am keen on the arrest of Arsène Lupin.

He escorted me to the automobile. Two of his agents, whom he introduced to me, Honoré Massol and Gaston Delivet, took their seats inside. I settled in at the wheel. My mechanic cranked the engine. A few seconds later, we were leaving the station. I was saved.

Ah! I admit that as I drove along the boulevards surrounding the old Norman city, with the powerful engine of my thirty-five horsepower Moreau-Lepton, I felt a sense of pride. The engine purred harmoniously. On the right and left, the trees rushed past us. And now free, out of danger, I only had to take care of my personal matters, with the help of the two honest representatives of law enforcement. Arsène Lupin was off in search of Arsène Lupin!

Modest supporters of social order, Gaston Delivet and Honoré Massol, how invaluable your assistance was to me! What would I have done without you? Without you, how many times at the crossroads would I have chosen the wrong path! Without you, Arsène Lupin would have been mistaken, and the other would have escaped!

But everything was not finished. Far from it. I still had to catch up with the individual, and then retrieve the documents he had stolen from me. At all costs, I had to prevent my two accomplices from getting their noses into those papers, let alone seizing them. I wanted to use them while acting independently of them, and that was not easy.

In Darnétal, we arrived three minutes after the train had passed. I was consoled to learn that a man in a gray overcoat, with a velvet collar, had boarded a second-class compartment, holding a ticket to Amiens. Clearly, my beginnings as a policeman were promising.

Delivet said to me:

—The train is an express and will only stop again at Montérolier-Buchy in nineteen minutes. If we don't get there before Arsène Lupin, he could continue on to Amiens, or divert to Clères, and from there head to Dieppe or Paris.

—Montérolier, how far is it?

—Twenty-three kilometers.

—Twenty-three kilometers in nineteen minutes... We'll be there before him.

What an exhilarating leg of the journey! Never did my faithful Moreau-Lepton respond to my impatience with more fervor and precision. It seemed to me that I was transmitting my will to her directly, without the need for levers and controls. She shared my desires. She approved of my determination. She understood my animosity towards that scoundrel Arsène Lupin. That trickster! That traitor! Would I be able to outsmart him? Would he once again mock authority, the very authority of which I was the embodiment?

—To the right, shouted Delivet!... To the left!... Straight ahead!...

We glided above the ground. The markers appeared like timid little creatures that vanished at our approach.

And suddenly, around a bend in the road, a whirlwind of smoke, the Northern Express.

For a kilometer, it was a struggle, side by side, an unequal fight with a certain outcome. Upon arrival, we beat it by twenty lengths.

In three seconds, we were on the platform, in front of the second-class cars. The doors opened. A few people got off. My thief was gone. We searched the compartments. No Arsène Lupin.

"Goodness," I exclaimed, "he must have recognized me in the car while we were running side by side, and he jumped off."

The train conductor confirmed this assumption. He had seen a man tumbling down the embankment, two hundred meters from the station.

"Look, over there... the one crossing the level crossing."

I dashed forward, followed by my two accomplices, or rather by one of them, since the other, Massol, was an exceptional runner, having both endurance and speed. In no time, the distance between him and the fugitive significantly decreased. The man spotted him, jumped over a hedge, and quickly ran toward an embankment that he climbed. We could see him even further away: he was entering a small woods.

When we reached the woods, Massol was waiting for us there. He had deemed it unnecessary to venture further, fearing he might lose us.

"And I congratulate you, my dear friend," I said to him. "After such a run, our individual must be out of breath. We have him."

I surveyed the surroundings while contemplating how to proceed with the arrest of the fugitive on my own, in order to secure evidence that justice would likely have only tolerated after much unpleasant investigation. Then I returned to my companions.

—There you go, it's easy. You, Massol, take your position on the left. You, Delivet, go to the right. From there, you will watch the entire back line of the thicket, and no one can come out without you noticing, except through this opening, where I will take my position. If he doesn't come out, I'll go in, and inevitably, I will drive him toward one of you. So all you have to do is wait. Ah! I almost forgot: in case of an alert, one shot.

Massol and Delivet moved away in opposite directions. As soon as they disappeared, I entered the woods with the utmost caution, making sure to be neither seen nor heard. It was dense underbrush, arranged for hunting, intersected by very narrow paths where one could only walk bent over, like in green tunnels.

One of these paths led to a clearing where the wet grass showed signs of footsteps. I followed them, carefully slipping through the bushes. They led me to the foot of a small mound topped by a half-demolished plaster shack.

—He must be there, I thought. The observation point is well chosen.

I crawled close to the building. A slight noise alerted me to his presence, and indeed, through an opening, I saw him with his back turned to me.

In two leaps, I was on him. He tried to aim the revolver he held in his hand. I didn't give him the chance and dragged him to the ground, pinning his arms beneath him, twisted, while I pressed my knee against his chest.

—Listen, my little friend, I whispered in his ear, I am Arsène Lupin. You are going to give me, right now and willingly, my wallet and the lady's bag... in exchange for which I will pull you from the clutches of the police and recruit you among my friends. Just one word: yes or no?

—Yes, he murmured.

—That's good. Your business this morning was nicely arranged. We'll come to an agreement.

I stood up. He rummaged in his pocket, pulled out a large knife, and tried to strike me.

—Idiot! I shouted.

With one hand, I deflected the attack. With the other, I delivered a powerful blow to his carotid artery, a move known as the "carotid hook." He fell, dazed.

In my wallet, I found my papers and my banknotes. Out of curiosity, I took his. On an envelope addressed to him, I read his name: Pierre Onfrey.

I shuddered. Pierre Onfrey, the murderer from Rue Lafontaine in Auteuil! Pierre Onfrey, the one who had slaughtered Mme Delbois and his two daughters. I leaned over him. Yes, it was that face which, in the compartment, had evoked in me the memory of features I had already seen.

But time was passing. I placed two hundred-franc notes in an envelope, along with a card that read: "Arsène Lupin to his good colleagues Honoré Massol and Gaston Delivet, in token of appreciation." I left it prominently in the middle of the room. Next to it was Mme Renaud's bag. Could I not return it to the excellent friend who had helped me? I confess, however, that I took everything of any interest from it, leaving only a tortoiseshell comb, a Dorin red lipstick stick, and an empty wallet. What the hell! Business is business. And besides, her husband truly had such an unworthy profession!...

Then there was the man. He was starting to stir. What should I do? I had neither the right to save him nor to condemn him.

I took away his weapons and fired a shot into the air.

"The other two will come, I thought, let him manage! Things will unfold according to his destiny.

And I hurried away along the path of the dell.

Twenty minutes later, a side road that I had noticed during our chase brought me back to my car.

At four o'clock, I sent a telegram to my friends in Rouen informing them that an unexpected incident forced me to postpone my visit. Between us, I am quite afraid, given what they must know now, that I will have to postpone it indefinitely. A cruel disappointment for them!

At six o'clock, I returned to Paris via Isle-Adam, Enghien, and the Porte Bineau.

The evening newspapers informed me that they had finally succeeded in capturing Pierre Onfrey.

The next day—let's not overlook the benefits of clever publicity—L'Écho de France published this sensational snippet:

"Yesterday, in the vicinity of Buchy, after numerous incidents, Arsène Lupin arrested Pierre Onfrey. The assassin from Rue Lafontaine had just robbed Mme Renaud, the wife of the deputy director of penitentiary services, along the Paris to Le Havre line. Arsène Lupin returned to Mme Renaud the handbag containing her jewelry and generously rewarded the two security agents who assisted him during this dramatic arrest."

CHAPTER FIVE
THE QUEEN'S NECKLACE

Two or three times a year, on the occasion of significant events, such as the balls at the Austrian embassy or Lady Billingstone's soirées, Countess de Dreux-Soubise would adorn her white shoulders with "the Queen's Necklace."

It was indeed the famous necklace, the legendary necklace that Böhmer and Bassenge, crown jewelers, intended for Du Barry, which Cardinal de Rohan-Soubise believed he was offering to Marie-Antoinette, Queen of France, and which the adventurer Jeanne de Valois, Countess de la Motte, dismantled one evening in February 1785, with the help of her husband and their accomplice Rétaux de Villette.

To be truthful, only the setting was authentic. Rétaux de Villette had kept it, while the sieur de la Motte and his wife scattered the brutally removed stones to the four winds, the magnificent stones that Böhmer had so carefully chosen. Later, in Italy, he sold it to Gaston de Dreux-Soubise, the nephew and heir of the cardinal, who had been saved from ruin by his uncle during the notorious bankruptcy of Rohan-Guéménée. In memory of his uncle, he bought back the few diamonds that remained in the possession of the English jeweler Jefferys, supplemented them with others of much lesser value but of similar size, and managed to reconstruct the marvelous "necklace in bondage," just as it had come from the hands of Böhmer and Bassenge.

For nearly a century, the Dreux-Soubise family took pride in this historical jewel. Although various circumstances had significantly diminished their fortune, they preferred to cut back on their lifestyle rather than part with the royal and precious relic. In particular, the current count cherished it as one cherishes the home of their ancestors. As a precaution, he had rented a safe at Crédit Lyonnais to store it. He was going to retrieve it himself on the afternoon of the day his wife wanted to wear it, and he would return it himself the following day.

That evening, at the reception at the Palace of Castile, the countess was a true success, and King Christian, in whose honor the celebration was held, noticed her magnificent beauty. Jewels cascaded around her graceful neck. The thousand facets of the diamonds sparkled and glittered like flames in the light of the lamps. No one else, it seemed, could have worn such a burden of adornment with as much ease and nobility.

It was a double triumph that the Count of Dreux savored deeply, and he congratulated himself when they returned to their room in their old hotel in the Saint-Germain district. He was proud of his wife, and perhaps just as much of the jewel that had adorned his family for four generations. His wife derived a somewhat childish vanity from it, but it was indeed a mark of her haughty character.

With some regret, she unfastened the necklace from her shoulders and handed it to her husband, who examined it with admiration, as if he had never seen it before. Then, after placing it back in its red leather case emblazoned with the Cardinal's coat of arms, he went into a nearby cabinet, a sort of alcove that had been completely isolated from the room, with its only entrance at the foot of their bed. As he had done on previous occasions, he hid it on a high shelf among hat boxes and piles of linen. He closed the door and undressed.

In the morning, he got up around nine o'clock, intending to go to the Crédit Lyonnais before breakfast. He dressed, had a cup of coffee, and went down to the stables. There, he gave some orders. One of the horses was troubling him. He had it walk and trot in front of him in the courtyard. Then he returned to his wife.

She had not left the room and was doing her hair with the help of her maid. She said to him:

—You're going out!

—Yes... for this errand...

—Ah! indeed... that's more prudent...

He entered the room. But after a few seconds, he asked, without the slightest surprise:

—Did you take it, dear friend?

She replied:

—What? No, I didn't take anything.

—You disturbed it.

—Not at all... I didn't even open that door.

He appeared, disheveled, and stammered, his voice barely intelligible:

—You didn't...? It's not you...? Then...

She rushed over, and they searched feverishly, throwing boxes to the ground and demolishing piles of laundry. And the count kept repeating:

—It's useless… everything we're doing is useless… It's right here, on this shelf, where I put it.

—You might have made a mistake.

—It's right here, on this shelf, and not anywhere else.

They lit a candle, as the room was quite dim, and they removed all the laundry and objects that cluttered it. And when there was nothing left in the room, they had to admit in despair that the famous necklace, "the Queen's Enslavement Necklace," had disappeared.

Being resolute by nature, the countess, without wasting time on futile lamentations, had the commissioner, Mr. Valorbe, notified, whose keen intellect and insight they had already come to appreciate. They brought him up to speed in detail, and he immediately asked:

—Are you sure, Count, that no one could have crossed into your room during the night?

—Absolutely sure. I have very light sleep. Even better: the door to that room was locked. I must have locked it this morning when my wife rang for the maid.

—And is there no other way to access the room?

—None.

—No window?

—Yes, but it's boarded up.

—I would like to see for myself…

They lit some candles, and immediately Mr. Valorbe pointed out that the window was only blocked halfway up by a sideboard, which, moreover, did not fit snugly against the window frame.

—It fits close enough, replied Mr. de Dreux, that it would be impossible to move it without making a lot of noise.

—What does this window overlook?

—It looks out onto an inner courtyard.

—And do you have another floor above this one?

—Two, but at the level of the servants, the courtyard is protected by a small mesh grille. That's why we have so little light.

Besides, when they moved the sideboard, they found that the window was closed, which would not have been the case if someone had entered from the outside.

—Unless, the Count observed, that someone left through our room.

—In which case, you would not have found the lock on this room pushed.

The commissioner thought for a moment, then turned to the Countess:

—Did anyone in your circle, Madame, know that you were to wear this necklace last night?

—Certainly, I didn't hide it. But no one knew we were locking it in this cabinet.

—No one?

—No one... Unless...

—I beg you, Madame, please clarify. This is a very important point.

She said to her husband:

—I was thinking of Henriette.

—Henriette? She is unaware of this detail like the others.

—Are you sure of that?

—Who is this lady? Mr. Valorbe asked.

—A convent friend who fell out with her family to marry a sort of laborer. After her husband died, I took her and her son in and furnished an apartment for them in this hotel.

And she added, somewhat embarrassed:

—She does me a few favors. She is very skilled with her hands.

—What floor does she live on?

—Ours is not far from yours… at the end of this hallway… And actually, I just remembered… the window of her kitchen…

—It opens onto that little courtyard, doesn't it?

—Yes, right across from ours.

A brief silence followed this statement.

Then Mr. Valorbe requested to be taken to Henriette.

They found her sewing, while her son Raoul, a child of about six or seven, was reading beside her. Quite surprised by the miserable apartment that had been furnished for her—a single room without a fireplace and a small area serving as a kitchen—the commissioner began to question her. She appeared shaken upon learning about the theft. The night before, she had dressed the countess and fastened the necklace around her neck.

—Good Lord! she exclaimed, who would have ever told me?

—And you have no idea? Not the slightest doubt? It's possible that the culprit came through your room.

She laughed heartily, not even imagining that she could be suspected:

—But I never left my room! I never go out. And besides, didn't you see?

She opened the window of the small area.

—Look, it's a good three meters to the opposite ledge.

—Who told you we were considering the possibility of a theft through there?

—But... wasn't the necklace in the cabinet?

—How do you know?

—Well! I always knew it was kept there at night... they talked about it in front of me...

Her face, still young but marked by sorrow, showed great gentleness and resignation. However, suddenly, in the silence, she had an expression of anxiety, as if a danger were threatening her. She pulled her son close to her. The child took her hand and kissed her tenderly.

"I don't suppose," said Mr. de Dreux to the commissioner when they were alone, "I don't suppose you suspect her, do you? I vouch for her. She is the very essence of honesty."

"Oh! I completely agree with you," affirmed Mr. Valorbe. "At most, I had considered the possibility of an unconscious complicity. But I acknowledge that this explanation must be discarded... especially since it does not resolve the problem we are facing."

The commissioner did not pursue this investigation further, as the investigating judge took it up and added to it in the following days. The servants were questioned, the state of the lock was checked, experiments were conducted on opening and closing the window of the study, and the courtyard was searched from top to bottom... Everything was in vain. The lock was intact. The window could neither be opened nor closed from the outside.

More specifically, the searches focused on Henriette, as, despite everything, attention always returned to her. Her life was thoroughly examined, and it was found that, for the past three years, she had only left the hotel four times, and those four times were for errands that could be accounted for. In reality, she served as a maid and seamstress for Madame de Dreux, who exhibited a strictness towards her that all the servants attested to in confidence.

—In fact, the examining judge said, after a week he reached the same conclusions as the commissioner, assuming we knew the culprit, which we do not, we would still not know any more about how the theft was committed. We are blocked on both sides by two obstacles: a closed door and a closed window. The mystery is twofold! How did someone manage to get in, and how, which is much more difficult, did they manage to escape while leaving behind a locked door and a closed window?

After four months of investigation, the judge's secret idea was this: Mr. and Mrs.me de Dreux, pressed by significant financial needs, had sold the Queen's Necklace. He closed the case.

The theft of the precious jewel dealt a blow to the Dreux-Soubise family that they would bear the marks of for a long time. Their credit, no longer supported by the kind of reserve that such a treasure represented, left them facing more demanding creditors and less favorable lenders. They had to cut deeply, sell off, and mortgage. In short, it would have been ruinous if two sizable inheritances from distant relatives hadn't saved them.

They also suffered in their pride, as if they had lost a quarter of their nobility. And strangely enough, it was against her former boarding school friend that the countess directed her ire. She felt a genuine resentment towards her and openly accused her. First, she was relegated to the servants' quarters, then she was dismissed overnight.

And life went on, without notable events. They traveled a lot.

Only one fact should be highlighted during this time. A few months after Henriette's departure, the countess received a letter from her that filled her with astonishment:

"Madam,

"I don't know how to thank you. It is indeed you, isn't it, who sent me this? It can only be you. No one else knows my hiding place in this small village. If I am mistaken, please forgive me, but at least accept my expression of gratitude for your past kindness..."

What did she mean? The countess's current or past kindnesses towards her amounted to many injustices. What did these thanks signify?

Pressed to explain, she replied that she had received, by mail, in an unregistered and unmarked envelope, two notes of one thousand francs each. The envelope, which she attached to her response, was postmarked from Paris and bore only her address, written in a clearly disguised hand.

Where did these two thousand francs come from? Who had sent them? Justice inquired. But what lead could be followed in this darkness?

And the same event occurred again twelve months later. And a third time; and a fourth time; and every year for six years, with the difference that in the fifth and sixth years, the amount doubled, allowing Henriette, who suddenly fell ill, to receive proper treatment.

Another difference: the postal administration seized one of the letters on the grounds that it was unregistered, so the last two letters were sent according to regulations, one dated from Saint-Germain and the other from Suresnes. The sender first signed as Anquety, then as Péchard. The addresses he provided were false.

After six years, Henriette died. The mystery remained unsolved.

* * *

All these events are known to the public. The case was one that captivated public opinion, and it is a strange fate for this necklace, which, after causing such turmoil in France at the end of the eighteenth century, stirred up so much emotion a century later. However, what I am about to reveal is unknown to everyone except the main parties involved and a few individuals to whom the count requested absolute secrecy. Since it is likely that sooner or later they will break their promise, I have no qualms about tearing the veil, and in doing so, we will have not only the key to the mystery but also the explanation of the letter published by the newspapers the day before yesterday—a remarkable letter that added, if possible, even more shadow and mystery to the obscurities of this drama.

This happened five days ago. Among the guests who were having lunch at Mr. de Dreux-Soubise's were his two nieces and his cousin, and among the men were the president of Essaville, Deputy Bochas, Chevalier Floriani, whom the count had met in Sicily, and General Marquis de Rouzières, an old friend from their social circle.

After the meal, the ladies served coffee, and the gentlemen were allowed a cigarette, on the condition that they did not leave the salon. They chatted. One of the young women entertained herself by reading cards and telling fortunes. Then they began to discuss famous crimes. It was in this context that Mr. de Rouzières, who never missed an opportunity to tease the count, brought up the story of the necklace— a topic that Mr. de Dreux despised.

Immediately, everyone offered their opinions. Each person restarted the investigation in their own way. And, of course, all the hypotheses contradicted each other, all equally implausible.

—And you, sir, asked the Countess of the Chevalier Floriani, what is your opinion?

—Oh! I have no opinion, madam.

There was an outcry. The Chevalier had just recounted various adventures he had experienced with his father, a magistrate in Palermo, where his judgment and taste for such matters had been demonstrated.

—I admit, he said, that I have succeeded when more skilled individuals have given up. But to consider myself a Sherlock Holmes... And besides, I barely know what this is about.

Everyone turned to the master of the house. Reluctantly, he had to summarize the facts. The Chevalier listened, thought, asked a few questions, and murmured:

—This is funny... at first glance, it doesn't seem to me that this is so difficult to deduce.

The Count shrugged. But the others hurried around the Chevalier, and he resumed with a somewhat dogmatic tone:

—Generally, to trace back to the author of a crime or a theft, one must determine how that crime or theft was committed, or at least how it could have been committed. In the current case, it seems quite simple to me, because we are faced not with several hypotheses, but with a certainty, a unique, rigorous certainty, which can be stated as follows: the individual could only have entered through the door of the room or through the window of the study. Now, one does not open a locked door from the outside. Therefore, he must have entered through the window.

—It was closed, and it was found closed, Mr. de Dreux stated clearly.

—For that, continued Floriani without acknowledging the interruption, he only needed to establish a bridge, plank, or ladder between the kitchen balcony and the window ledge, and as soon as the case...

—But I repeat to you that the window was closed! the count exclaimed impatiently.

This time, Floriani had to respond. He did so with the utmost calm, like a man who is not disturbed by such an insignificant objection.

—I want to believe that it was, but isn't there a small window?

—How do you know?

—First of all, it's almost a rule in hotels of this era. And secondly, it must be the case, since otherwise, the theft is inexplicable.

—Indeed, there is one, but it was closed, just like the window. No one even paid attention to it.

—That's a mistake. Because if someone had noticed, they would have clearly seen that it had been opened.

—And how?

—I assume that, like all the others, it opens with a twisted wire, equipped with a ring at its lower end?

—Yes.

—And that ring was hanging between the window and the sideboard?

—Yes, but I don't understand…

—Here's how. Through a gap made in the glass, one could have used some tool, let's say a metal rod with a hook, to grab the ring, pull, and open it.

The count scoffed:

—Perfect! Perfect! You arrange all this with such ease! Only you forget one thing, dear sir, which is that there was no gap made in the glass.

—There was a gap.

—Come now! It would have been seen.

—To see, one must look, and no one looked. The gap exists; it is materially impossible for it not to exist, along the glass, against the putty... in the vertical direction, of course...

The count stood up. He seemed very agitated. He paced back and forth across the room several times, and, approaching Floriani:

—Nothing has changed up there since that day... no one has set foot in that room.

—In that case, sir, you are free to ensure that my explanation aligns with reality.

—It does not align with any of the facts that justice has established. You have seen nothing, you know nothing, and you are going against everything we have seen and everything we know.

Floriani did not seem to notice the count's irritation and said with a smile:

—My goodness, sir, I am simply trying to see clearly, that's all. If I am mistaken, prove me wrong.

—Without further delay... I admit that your confidence, over time...

Mr. de Dreux mumbled a few more words, then suddenly turned towards the door and left.

Not a word was spoken. They waited anxiously, as if, indeed, a piece of the truth was about to emerge. The silence was extremely grave.

Finally, the count appeared in the doorway. He was pale and unusually agitated. He said to his friends in a trembling voice:

—I apologize... the revelations from this gentleman are so unexpected... I never would have thought...

His wife eagerly questioned him:

—Speak... I beg you... what is it?

He stammered:

—The crack exists... exactly where indicated... along the tile...

He suddenly grabbed the knight's arm and said in an imperative tone:

—And now, sir, continue... I acknowledge that you have been right up to this point, but now... It's not over... answer me... what happened in your view?

Floriani gently freed himself and after a moment said:

—Well, in my opinion, here's what happened. The individual, knowing that Mme from Dreux was going to the ball with the necklace, set up his access point during your absence. Through the window, he watched you and saw you hide the jewelry. As soon as you left, he broke the glass and took the ring.

—That may be, but the distance is too great for him to have reached the window handle through the skylight.

—If he couldn't open it, then he must have entered through the skylight itself.

—Impossible; there isn't a person slim enough to get through there.

—Then it's not a person.

—What do you mean?

—Certainly. If the passage is too narrow for a man, it must be a child.

—A child!

—Did you not tell me that your friend Henriette had a son?

—Indeed... a son named Raoul.

—It is highly probable that this Raoul is the one who committed the theft.

—What proof do you have?

—What proof!... there is no lack of evidence... For example...

He fell silent and thought for a few seconds. Then he continued:

—For example, it is not believable that the child brought that access point from outside and took it away without anyone noticing. He must have used what was available to him. In the small room where Henriette did her cooking, there were, if I recall correctly, shelves mounted on the wall for placing pots?

—Two shelves, as far as I remember.

—We need to check if those shelves are actually secured to the wooden supports that hold them. If not, we would be justified in thinking that the child pried them off and then connected them together. Perhaps also, since there was a stove, we might find the stove hook that he must have used to open the skylight.

Without a word, the count left, and this time the attendees felt none of the slight anxiety of the unknown that they had experienced the first time. They knew, they knew absolutely, that Floriani's predictions were correct. There was an impression of such unwavering certainty emanating from this man that he was not listened to as if he were deducing facts from one another, but as if he were recounting events whose authenticity could easily be verified as they unfolded.

And no one was surprised when the count declared upon his return:

—It's the child, it's definitely him; everything confirms it.

—You saw the boards... the hook?

—I saw... the boards have been pried loose... the hook is still there.

But Mme de Dreux-Soubise exclaimed:

—It's him... You mean it's his mother. Henriette is the only guilty one. She must have coerced her son...

—No, the knight affirmed, the mother is not to blame.

—Come now! They lived in the same room; the child could not have acted without Henriette knowing.

—They lived in the same room, but everything happened in the next room, at night, while the mother was asleep.

—And the necklace? the count asked, it would have been found among the child's belongings.

—Excuse me! He was leaving. The very morning you caught him at his work desk, he had just come from school, and perhaps justice, instead of exhausting its resources against the innocent mother, would have been better advised to search over there, in the child's desk, among his schoolbooks.

—Fair enough, but those two thousand francs that Henriette received every year, isn't that the best sign of her complicity?

—Complice, would she have thanked you for that money? And weren't they watching her? While the child is free, he has every opportunity to run to the nearby town, to meet with some dealer and sell a diamond, two diamonds, as the case may be... on the sole condition that the money is sent from Paris, after which they will start again the following year.

An indefinable discomfort weighed on the Dreux-Soubise family and their guests. Truly, there was something in Floriani's tone and demeanor that went beyond the certainty which had irritated the count from the very beginning. There was a hint of irony, and an irony that seemed more hostile than sympathetic or friendly, as would have been appropriate.

The count pretended to laugh.

—All of this is so clever that it delights me; my compliments. What a brilliant imagination!

—No, no, Floriani exclaimed more seriously, I'm not imagining; I'm recalling circumstances that were inevitably as I describe them.

—How do you know?

—What you yourself told me. I picture the life of the mother and the child, back there in the depths of the province, the mother falling ill, the tricks and schemes of the little one to sell the jewels and save his mother or at least ease her last moments. The illness prevails. She dies. Years pass. The child grows up, becomes a man. And then—and this time, I'm willing to admit that my imagination is running wild—let's suppose this man feels the need to return to the places where he lived during his childhood, to see them again, to find those who suspected and accused his mother... can you imagine the poignant interest of such a meeting in the old house where the events of the drama took place?

His words echoed for a few seconds in the uneasy silence, and on the faces of Mr. and Mrs. me de Dreux, there was a desperate effort to understand, alongside the fear and anxiety of comprehension. The count murmured:

—Who are you, sir?

—Me? I am the Chevalier Floriani, whom you met in Palermo, and whom you have been kind enough to invite to your home several times.

—Then what does this story mean?

—Oh! it means nothing at all! It's just a little game on my part. I try to imagine the joy that Henriette's son, if he still exists, would feel in telling you that he was the only guilty one, and that he was because his mother was unhappy, on the verge of losing the position of...

servant that she lived off, and because the child suffered from seeing his mother in distress.

He spoke with contained emotion, half-risen and leaning toward the countess. There could be no doubt. The Chevalier Floriani was none other than Henriette's son. Everything about his demeanor and words proclaimed it. Moreover, wasn't it his evident intention, his very will, to be recognized as such?

The count hesitated. How should he respond to this audacious person? Call for help? Cause a scandal? Expose the one who had wronged him long ago? But it had been so long! And who would want to admit to this absurd story of a guilty child? No, it was better to accept the situation while pretending not to grasp its true meaning. And the count, approaching Floriani, exclaimed cheerfully:

—Very amusing, very curious, your story. I assure you, I find it captivating. But tell me, what has become of this good young man, this model son? I hope he hasn't stopped on such a fine path.

—Oh! certainly not.

"Isn't it so! After such a beginning! Taking the Queen's Necklace at the age of six, the famous necklace that Marie Antoinette coveted!"

"And taking it," Floriani observed, playing along with the count, "taking it without any inconvenience to himself, without anyone thinking to check the state of the tiles or noticing that the windowsill is too clean, the very windowsill he wiped to erase the traces of his passage on the thick dust... Admit that it would be enough to make a child his age dizzy. Is it really that easy? Is it just a matter of wanting it and reaching out?... Indeed, he wanted..."

"And he reached out his hand."

"Both hands," the knight interjected with a laugh.

There was a shiver. What mystery lay hidden in the life of this so-called Floriani? How extraordinary must be the existence of this adventurer, a brilliant thief at six years old, who now, with a dilettante's flair in search of excitement, or perhaps merely to satisfy a sense of resentment, dared to confront his victim at her own home, boldly, recklessly, yet with all the decorum of a gentleman on a visit!

He stood up and approached the countess to take his leave. She suppressed a flinch. He smiled.

"Oh! Madame, you are afraid! Have I perhaps pushed my little magician's act too far!"

She composed herself and replied with a slightly teasing nonchalance:

"Not at all, Monsieur. The tale of this good son has, on the contrary, greatly interested me, and I am pleased that my necklace provided the occasion for such a brilliant fate. But don't you think that the son of this... woman, this Henriette, was primarily following his calling?"

He flinched, sensing the jab, and replied:

—I am convinced of it, and it was necessary for this calling to be serious so that the child would not be discouraged.

—And how so?

—Well, you know that most of the stones were fake. Only a few diamonds bought from the English jeweler were real; the others had been sold off one by one due to the harsh necessities of life.

—It was always the Queen's Necklace, Sir, the countess said with hauteur, and it seems to me that this is what Henriette's son could not understand.

—He must have understood, Madam, that whether fake or real, the necklace was above all a display object, a symbol.

Mr. de Dreux made a gesture. His wife immediately interrupted him.

—Sir, she said, if the man you are referring to has any modesty...

She paused, intimidated by Floriani's calm gaze.

He repeated:

—If that man has any modesty...

She realized that speaking to him in this manner would gain her nothing, and despite herself, despite her anger and indignation, trembling with a sense of humiliated pride, she said to him almost politely:

—Sir, legend has it that Rétaux de Villette, when he had the Queen's Necklace in his hands and had removed all the diamonds with Jeanne de Valois, did not dare to touch the setting. He understood that the diamonds were merely adornments, accessories, but that the setting was the essential work, the very creation of the artist, and he respected it. Do you think that man understood this as well?

—I have no doubt that the setting exists. The child respected it.

—Well, Sir, if you happen to meet him, you will tell him that he unjustly keeps one of those relics that belong to and bring glory to certain families, and that he was able to tear the stones away without the Queen's Necklace ceasing to belong to the house of Dreux-Soubise. It belongs to us just like our name, like our honor.

The knight simply replied:

—I will tell him, Madame.

He bowed before her, saluted the count, greeted each of the guests one by one, and left.

* * *

Four days later, Mme de Dreux found on the table in his room a red leather case bearing the Cardinal's coat of arms. He opened it. It was the Queen's Necklace in bondage.

But as all things must, in the life of a man concerned with unity and logic, converge towards the same goal—and since a bit of publicity is never harmful—the next day Écho de France published these sensational lines:

"The Queen's Necklace, the famous historical jewel once stolen from the family of Dreux-Soubise, has been recovered by Arsène Lupin. Arsène Lupin hastened to return it to its rightful owners. One can only applaud this delicate and chivalrous gesture."

CHAPTER SIX
THE SEVEN OF HEARTS

A question arises, and it has often been posed to me:

—How did I come to know Arsène Lupin?

No one doubts that I know him. The details I gather about this perplexing man, the irrefutable facts I present, the new evidence I provide, the interpretation I give of certain actions that were only seen in their external manifestations without delving into their secret reasons or invisible mechanisms—all this clearly proves, if not an intimacy that Lupin's very existence would make impossible, at least friendly relations and ongoing confidences.

But how did I come to know him? Where does the favor of being his historian come from? Why me and not someone else?

The answer is simple: it was sheer chance that determined a choice in which my merit plays no role. It was chance that put me in his path. It was by chance that I became involved in one of his strangest and most mysterious adventures, and by chance that I became an actor in a drama in which he was the marvelous director—a dark and complex drama, filled with such twists that I feel a certain hesitation as I prepare to recount it.

The first act takes place during that famous night of June 22 to 23, which has been talked about so much. And for my part, let's say it right away, I attribute my rather unusual behavior that night to the very special state of mind I was in when I returned home. We had dined with friends at the Cascade restaurant, and all evening, while we smoked and the gypsy orchestra played melancholic waltzes, we had talked only of crimes and thefts, of frightening and dark intrigues. This is always a poor preparation for sleep.

The Saint-Martins left by car. Jean Daspry— that charming and carefree Daspry who would tragically be killed six months later at the Moroccan border—Jean Daspry and I walked back through the dark, warm night. When we arrived in front of the small hotel where I had been living for a year in Neuilly, on Boulevard Maillot, he said to me:

—Aren't you ever afraid?

—What an idea!

—Well, this building is so isolated! No neighbors... vacant lots... Honestly, I'm not a coward, and yet...

—Well, you are cheerful, aren't you!

—Oh! I say this as I would say anything else. The Saint-Martins impressed me with their stories of bandits.

After shaking my hand, he stepped away. I took my key and opened the door.

—Well then! I murmured, Antoine forgot to light a candle for me.

And suddenly I remembered: Antoine was absent; I had given him the day off.

Immediately, the shadow and silence became unpleasant. I climbed to my room as quickly as I could, feeling my way, and, contrary to my usual practice, I turned the key and bolted the door.

The flame of the candle restored my composure. Still, I made sure to draw my revolver from its holster, a large, long-range revolver, and I set it beside my bed. This precaution finally reassured me. I lay down, and as usual, to help me fall asleep, I picked up the book that awaited me on my nightstand each evening.

I was very surprised. Instead of the paper knife I had used as a bookmark the night before, there was an envelope, sealed with five red wax seals. I grabbed it quickly. It bore my name, along with the word: "Urgent."

A letter! A letter addressed to me! Who could have placed it there? A little anxious, I tore open the envelope and read:

"From the moment you open this letter, whatever happens, whatever you hear, do not move, do not make a sound, do not cry out. Otherwise, you are lost."

I am not a coward either, and just like anyone else, I know how to face real danger or to laugh at the imaginary perils that our minds conjure up. But, I repeat, I was in an abnormal state of mind, more easily impressionable, my nerves on edge. Besides, wasn't there something unsettling and inexplicable in all this that could shake the soul of even the bravest person?

My fingers gripped the piece of paper feverishly, and my eyes kept rereading the threatening phrases... "Do not make a move... do not scream... otherwise, you are lost..." Come on! I thought, this must be a joke, a silly prank.

I was about to laugh, in fact, I wanted to laugh out loud. What stopped me? What vague fear constricted my throat?

At least I could blow out the candle. No, I couldn't blow it out. "Not a move, or you are lost," it was written.

But why fight against these kinds of self-suggestions that are often more powerful than the most precise facts? I just had to close my eyes. I closed my eyes.

At that moment, a slight noise broke the silence, followed by some creaking. It seemed to be coming from a large room next door where I had set up my study, separated from it only by the antechamber.

The approach of real danger heightened my senses, and I felt as if I was going to get up, grab my revolver, and rush into that room. I did not get up: in front of me, one of the curtains of the left window had moved.

Doubt was not possible: it had moved. It was still moving! And I saw —oh! I saw this clearly—that there was a human shape between the curtains and the window, in that too narrow space, the thickness of which prevented the fabric from falling straight.

And the being could see me too; I was sure he could see me through the wide gaps in the fabric. Then I understood everything. While the others took their loot, his mission was to keep me in check. Get up? Grab a revolver? Impossible... he was there! At the slightest movement, at the faintest cry, I was lost.

A violent blow shook the house, followed by small knocks grouped in twos or threes, like those of a hammer striking nails and bouncing back. Or at least that's what I imagined, in the confusion of my mind. And other noises intertwined, a real racket that proved they were not being discreet, and that they were acting with complete assurance.

They were right: I did not move. Was it cowardice? No, rather annihilation, total inability to move even a single limb. Wisdom as well, for why fight? Behind this man, there were ten others who would come at his call. Was I going to risk my life to save a few tapestries and some trinkets?

And all through the night, this torment lasted. Intolerable torment, terrible anguish! The noise had stopped, but I kept waiting for it to start again. And the man! The man who was watching me, weapon in hand! My terrified gaze did not leave him. And my heart was pounding! Sweat was pouring down my forehead and all over my body!

And suddenly, an indescribable sense of well-being washed over me: a milkman's cart, whose sound I knew well, passed by on the boulevard, and at the same time, I felt as if dawn was slipping through the closed shutters, and a bit of daylight outside mingled with the shadows.

The day entered the room. Other carts passed by. And all the ghosts of the night vanished.

Then I slowly and stealthily extended one arm out of bed. Nothing stirred in front of me. I marked the crease of the curtain with my eyes, pinpointing exactly where I needed to aim. I calculated precisely the movements I needed to make, and quickly, I grabbed my revolver and fired.

I leaped out of bed with a cry of liberation and jumped at the curtain. The fabric was pierced, the glass was shattered. As for the man, I hadn't been able to hit him… for the simple reason that there was no one there.

No one! So, all night long, I had been hypnotized by a fold in the curtain! And in the meantime, criminals… Furiously, with a momentum that nothing could stop, I turned the key in the lock, opened my door, crossed the anteroom, opened another door, and rushed into the room.

But a shock froze me on the threshold, panting, stunned, more surprised than I had been by the absence of the man: nothing had disappeared. All the things I had assumed were taken—furniture, paintings, old velvet, and old silks—everything was in its place!

An incomprehensible spectacle! I couldn't believe my eyes! Yet the noise, the sounds of moving... I walked around the room, inspected the walls, and took stock of all the objects I knew so well. Nothing was missing! What puzzled me the most was that nothing revealed the presence of intruders; there were no clues, not a single chair out of place, no footprints.

"Come on, come on," I told myself, holding my head in my hands, "I can't be going crazy! I definitely heard something!..."

Inch by inch, using the most meticulous investigative techniques, I examined the room. It was in vain. Or rather... could I consider this a discovery? Under a small Persian rug thrown on the floor, I found a card, a playing card. It was a seven of hearts, just like all the sevens of hearts in French playing cards, but it caught my attention due to a rather curious detail. The very tip of each of the seven red heart marks was pierced with a hole, a round and regular hole that could only have been made by the end of a punch.

That was all. A card and a letter found in a book. Other than that, nothing. Was that enough to assert that I hadn't just been the plaything of a dream?

* * *

All day long, I continued my research in the lounge. It was a large room, disproportionately spacious compared to the cramped hotel, and its decor reflected the peculiar taste of its designer. The floor was made of a mosaic of small, multicolored stones, creating broad symmetrical patterns. The same mosaic adorned the walls, arranged in panels depicting Pompeian allegories, Byzantine compositions, and medieval frescoes. A Bacchus was riding a barrel. An emperor, crowned in gold and sporting a flowery beard, held a sword in his right hand.

At the very top, resembling a workshop, there was a single large window. Since this window was always left open at night, it was likely that someone had entered through it using a ladder. Yet, there was still no certainty. The rungs of the ladder should have left marks on the beaten ground of the courtyard, but there were none. The grass in the vacant lot surrounding the hotel should have been freshly trampled, but it was not.

I admit that I never thought to contact the police, as the facts I would have needed to present were so inconsistent and absurd. They would have laughed at me. However, the day after next was my day to write a column for Gil Blas, where I was working at the time. Obsessed with my experience, I recounted it in detail.

The article did not go unnoticed, but I could tell that it was not taken seriously and was regarded more as a fanciful tale than a true story. The Saint-Martins mocked me. However, Daspry, who had some expertise in these matters, came to see me, asked for an explanation of the situation, and studied it… but with no more success, it must be said.

One of the following mornings, the bell at the gate rang, and Antoine came to inform me that a gentleman wanted to speak with me. He had not wanted to give his name. I asked him to come up.

It was a man in his forties, very dark-haired, with an energetic face, and his clean but worn clothes indicated a concern for elegance that contrasted with his rather vulgar manners.

Without preamble, he said to me—in a hoarse voice, with accents that confirmed the man's social standing:

—Sir, while traveling, I came across your article in a café, the Gil Blas. I found it… very interesting.

—Thank you.

—And I came back.

—Oh!

—Yes, to speak with you. Are all the facts you recounted accurate?

—Absolutely accurate.

—Is there not a single one that you invented?

—Not a single one.

—In that case, I may have some information to provide you.

—I'm listening.

—No.

—What do you mean, no?

—Before I speak, I need to verify if they are correct.

—And to verify them?

—I need to be alone in this room.

I looked at him in surprise.

—I don't quite understand…

—It's an idea I had while reading your article. Certain details establish an extraordinary coincidence with another adventure that chance revealed to me. If I'm mistaken, it's better for me to remain silent. And the only way to know is for me to be alone…

What was behind this proposition? Later, I recalled that when he made it, the man had a worried look, an anxious expression. But at the moment, although a bit taken aback, I found nothing particularly unusual about his request. And such curiosity piqued my interest!

I replied:

—Alright. How much time do you need?

—Oh! Just three minutes, no more. In three minutes, I will join you.

I left the room. Downstairs, I checked my watch. One minute passed. Two minutes... Why did I feel so anxious? Why did these moments seem more serious than others?

Two and a half minutes... Two minutes and three-quarters... And suddenly, a gunshot rang out.

In a few strides, I rushed up the stairs and entered. A scream of horror escaped me.

In the middle of the room, the man lay still, on his left side. Blood flowed from his head, mixed with fragments of brain. Near his fist, a revolver, still smoking.

He was seized by a convulsion, and that was all.

But more than this horrifying sight, something struck me, something that made me not call for help right away, and kept me from dropping to my knees to check if the man was breathing. Two steps away from him, on the floor, there was a seven of hearts!

I picked it up. The seven points of the seven red marks had holes in them...

* * *

Half an hour later, the police commissioner from Neuilly arrived, then the coroner, and finally the head of the Security, Mr. Dudouis. I had carefully refrained from touching the corpse. Nothing could distort the initial findings.

They were brief, all the more so because at first, nothing was discovered, or very little. In the dead man's pockets, there was no paper; on his clothes, no name; on his linen, no initials. In short, there was not a single clue capable of establishing his identity. And in the room, everything was as it had been before. The furniture had not been disturbed, and the objects retained their previous positions. Yet this man did not come to my home solely with the intention of killing himself, believing that my house was better suited than any other for his suicide! There must have been a reason that drove him to this act of despair, and that reason itself must have stemmed from something new he had witnessed during the three minutes he spent alone.

What fact? What had he seen? What had he stumbled upon? What dreadful secret had he uncovered? No conjecture was allowed.

But, at the last moment, an incident occurred that seemed to us of considerable interest. As two officers bent down to lift the corpse and carry it out on a stretcher, they noticed that the left hand, which had been clenched and tense until then, had relaxed, and a crumpled business card slipped out.

The card read: Georges Andermatt, 37 rue de Berry.

What did this mean? Georges Andermatt was a prominent banker in Paris, the founder and president of the Comptoir des métaux, which had given great momentum to the metallurgical industries in France. He lived lavishly, owning a mail-coach, automobiles, and a racing stable. His gatherings were well-attended, and Mme Andermatt was noted for his charm and good looks.

"Could this be the name of the deceased?" I murmured.

The head of the Security Service leaned in.

"It is not him. Mr. Andermatt is a pale man with a bit of gray."

—But then why this card?

—Do you have a phone, sir?

—Yes, in the hallway. If you would be so kind as to accompany me.

He looked in the directory and dialed 415.21.

—Is Mr. Andermatt at home? —Please tell him that Mr. Dudouis requests him to come urgently to 102 Boulevard Maillot. It's urgent.

Twenty minutes later, Mr. Andermatt stepped out of his car. The reasons for his needed intervention were explained, and then he was taken to see the body.

He had a moment of emotional contraction that twisted his face, and he whispered, as if involuntarily:

—Étienne Varin.

—Did you know him?

—No... or rather yes... but only by sight. His brother...

—He has a brother?

—Yes, Alfred Varin... His brother once came to solicit me... I can't remember for what reason...

—Where does he live?

—The two brothers lived together... on Rue de Provence, I believe.

—And you don't suspect the reason why he killed himself?

—Not at all.

—However, this card he was holding in his hand?... Your card with your address!

—I don't understand it. It's obviously just a coincidence that the investigation will clarify for us.

A curious coincidence in any case, I thought, and I felt that we all shared the same impression.

I found this impression echoed in the newspapers the next day, and in conversations with all my friends with whom I discussed the incident. Amid the mysteries complicating it, after the double discovery, so bewildering, of that seven of hearts pierced seven times, after the two equally enigmatic events that had taken place in my home, this business card seemed to finally promise a bit of clarity. Through it, we would arrive at the truth.

But, contrary to expectations, Mr. Andermatt provided no information.

"I've said what I know," he repeated. "What more do you want? I am as surprised as anyone that this map was found there, and I am waiting, like everyone else, for this point to be clarified."

It was not clarified. The investigation revealed that the Varin brothers, of Swiss origin, had led a very tumultuous life under different names, frequenting gambling houses and associating with a group of foreigners that the police were monitoring, who had scattered after a series of burglaries in which their involvement was only established later. At number 24, Rue de Provence, where the Varin brothers had indeed lived six years earlier, no one knew what had become of them.

I confess that, for my part, this case seemed so tangled that I hardly believed a solution was possible, and I tried not to think about it anymore. But Jean Daspry, on the contrary, whom I saw often during that time, became increasingly passionate about it each day.

It was he who drew my attention to this snippet from a foreign newspaper that the entire press was reproducing and commenting on:

"They will proceed in the presence of the emperor, and in a location that will be kept secret until the last minute, with the first trials of a submarine that is set to revolutionize future naval warfare. An indiscretion has revealed its name: it is called The Seven of Hearts."

The Seven of Hearts! Was this a mere coincidence? Or should a connection be established between the name of this submarine and the incidents we have discussed? But what kind of connection? What was happening here could not possibly be linked to what was happening over there.

—What do you know? Daspry said to me. The most disparate effects often arise from a single cause.

The day after tomorrow, another echo reached us:

"It is claimed that the plans for the Seven of Hearts, the submarine whose experiments are set to take place imminently, were executed by French engineers. These engineers, having unsuccessfully sought support from their compatriots, then turned to the British Admiralty, also without success. We present this news with all due reservations."

I hesitate to dwell too much on matters of an extremely delicate nature, which, as we remember, caused considerable emotion. However, since any risk of complications has been dismissed, I must address the article from the Écho de France, which made quite a stir and shed some... albeit confusing light on the Seven of Hearts affair, as it was called.

Here it is, as it appeared under the signature of Salvator:

The Seven of Hearts Affair: A Corner of the Veil Lifted.

"We will be brief. Ten years ago, a young mining engineer, Louis Lacombe, eager to dedicate his time and fortune to his studies, resigned and rented a small hotel at 102 Boulevard Maillot, recently built and decorated by an Italian count. Through the intermediary of two individuals, the Varin brothers from Lausanne—one assisting him in his experiments as a technician, while the other sought sponsors for him—he established connections with H. Georges Andermatt, who had just founded the Comptoir des Métaux."

"After several meetings, he managed to interest him in a submarine project he was working on, and it was agreed that once the invention was fully developed, Mr. Andermatt would use his influence to obtain a series of trials from the Ministry of the Navy.

"For two years, Louis Lacombe frequented the Andermatt hotel regularly and presented the banker with the improvements he was making to his project, until the day when, satisfied with his work and having found the definitive formula he was searching for, he asked Mr. Andermatt to get things moving.

"That day, Louis Lacombe dined at the Andermatt's. He left in the evening around eleven-thirty. Since then, he has not been seen again.

"Upon rereading the newspapers from that time, one would see that the young man's family took legal action and that the public prosecutor became concerned. However, no certainty was reached, and it was generally accepted that Louis Lacombe, who was seen as an original and whimsical young man, had gone on a trip without telling anyone.

"Let's accept this... unlikely hypothesis. But one crucial question arises for our country: what happened to the submarine plans? Did Louis Lacombe take them with him? Are they destroyed?"

"From the very serious investigation we conducted, it turns out that these plans exist. The Varin brothers had them in their possession. How? We have not yet been able to establish that, just as we do not know why they did not try to sell them earlier. Were they afraid someone would ask how they obtained them? In any case, that fear did not last, and we can confidently state this: the plans of Louis Lacombe are the property of a foreign power, and we are prepared to publish the correspondence exchanged regarding this matter between the Varin brothers and the representative of that power.

Currently, the Sept-de-cœur envisioned by Louis Lacombe is being realized by our neighbors.

"Will reality meet the optimistic expectations of those involved in this betrayal? We have reasons to hope otherwise, and we would like to believe that events will not deceive us."

And a postscript added:

"Breaking news.—We had hoped rightly. Our specific information allows us to announce that the tests of the Sept-de-cœur have not been satisfactory. It is quite likely that the plans delivered by the Varin brothers were missing the final document brought by Louis Lacombe to Mr. Andermatt on the evening of his disappearance, a document essential for the complete understanding of the project, a sort of summary containing the final conclusions, evaluations, and measurements found in the other papers. Without this document, the plans are incomplete; just as, without the plans, the document is worthless."

"Therefore, there is still time to take action and reclaim what belongs to us. For this very difficult task, we rely heavily on Mr. Andermatt's assistance. He will be keen to explain the inexplicable behavior he has exhibited from the beginning. He will say not only why he did not share what he knew at the time of Étienne Varin's suicide, but also why he never revealed the disappearance of the documents he was aware of. He will explain why, for the past six years, he has had the Varin brothers monitored by agents in his employ.

"We expect from him not just words, but actions. Otherwise..."

The threat was harsh. But what did it entail? What means of intimidation did Salvator, the anonymous author of the article, have over Mr. Andermatt?

A swarm of reporters surrounded the banker, and ten interviews reflected the disdain with which he responded to this ultimatum. In response, the correspondent from L'Écho de France wrote these three lines:

"Whether Mr. Andermatt likes it or not, he is now our collaborator in the endeavor we are undertaking."

* * *

On the day this reply was published, Daspry and I had dinner together. In the evening, with newspapers spread out on my table, we discussed the matter and examined it from every angle, feeling the irritation one would feel from endlessly walking in the shadows and constantly bumping into the same obstacles.

And suddenly, without my servant having warned me, without the bell having rung, the door opened, and a lady entered, covered by a thick veil.

I immediately stood up and approached her. She said to me:

—Are you the one, sir, who lives here?

—Yes, madam, but I must admit…

—The gate on the boulevard wasn't closed, she explained.

—But what about the vestibule door?"

She didn't reply, and I thought she must have taken the service staircase. So she knew the way?

There was a somewhat awkward silence. She looked at Daspry. Despite myself, as I would have done in a salon, I introduced him. Then I asked her to sit down and explain the purpose of her visit.

She removed her veil, and I saw that she had brown hair, a regular face, and while she wasn't very beautiful, she possessed an infinite charm, particularly from her serious and sorrowful eyes.

She simply said:

—I am Mrs. me Andermatt.

—Mrs. Andermatt! I repeated, increasingly surprised.

A new silence. And she continued in a calm voice, with the most serene demeanor:

—I come regarding that matter… that you know about. I thought perhaps I could obtain some information from you…

—My God, madam, I know no more than what has been reported in the newspapers. Please specify how I can assist you.

—I don't know… I don't know…

Only then did I sense that her calm was feigned, and beneath her facade of perfect security lay great distress. We remained silent, equally uncomfortable.

But Daspry, who had not stopped observing her, approached and said:

—May I ask you a few questions, madam?

—Oh! yes, she exclaimed, this way I will speak.

—You will speak… no matter what those questions are?

—No matter what they are.

He thought for a moment and asked:

—Did you know Louis Lacombe?

—Yes, through my husband.

—When did you see him for the last time?

—The evening he dined at our house.

—That evening, was there anything that made you think you would not see him again?

—No. He did mention a trip to Russia, but it was so vague!

—So you were planning to see him again?

—The day after tomorrow, for dinner.

—And how do you explain his disappearance?

—I can't explain it.

—And Mr. Andermatt?

—I don't know.

—However…

—Please don't question me about that.

—The article in L'Écho de France seems to suggest…

—What it seems to suggest is that the Varin brothers are not unrelated to this disappearance.

—Is that your opinion?

—Yes.

—On what do you base your conviction?

—When Louis Lacombe left, he was carrying a briefcase that contained all the documents related to his project. Two days later, there was a meeting between my husband and one of the Varin brothers, the one who is alive, during which my husband acquired proof that those documents were in the hands of the two brothers.

—And he didn't report them?

—No.

—Why?

—Because, in the briefcase, there was something other than Louis Lacombe's papers.

—What?

She hesitated, was about to answer, then ultimately remained silent. Daspry continued:

—So that's why your husband, without notifying the police, had the two brothers watched. He hoped to recover both the papers and that... compromising thing with which the two brothers were blackmailing him.

—Him... and me.

—Oh! You too?

—Mainly me.

She pronounced those three words in a muffled voice. Daspry observed her, took a few steps, and then returned to her:

—Did you write to Louis Lacombe?

—Of course... my husband was in contact...

—Aside from those official letters, didn't you write to Louis Lacombe... other letters? I apologize for my insistence, but it's essential that I know the whole truth. Did you write other letters?

Blushing, she murmured:

—Yes.

—And those are the letters that the Varin brothers possessed?

—Yes.

—So Mr. Andermatt knows about them?

—He hasn't seen them, but Alfred Varin revealed their existence to him, threatening to publish them if my husband acted against them. My husband was afraid... he backed down in the face of the scandal.

—Yet he did everything he could to seize those letters from them.

—He did everything he could... at least, I assume so, because after that last meeting with Alfred Varin, and after the few very harsh words he told me about it, there has been no intimacy or trust between my husband and me. We live like two strangers.

—In that case, if you have nothing to lose, what do you fear?

—No matter how indifferent I have become to him, I am the one he loved, the one he could still love;—oh! I am certain of this, she murmured in a passionate voice, he would have loved me again if he hadn't gotten hold of those cursed letters...

—What! He would have succeeded... But the two brothers were at odds, weren't they?

—Yes, and they even boasted, it seems, of having a safe hiding place.

—So?...

—I have every reason to believe that my husband discovered this hiding place!

—Come on! Where was it?

—Here.

I jumped.

—Here!

—Yes, and I had always suspected it. Louis Lacombe, very clever and passionate about mechanics, used to spend his spare time making chests and locks. The Varin brothers must have stumbled upon and later used one of those hiding places to conceal the letters... and probably other things as well.

—But they didn't live here, I exclaimed.

—Until your arrival four months ago, this pavilion remained unoccupied. It is therefore likely that they were planning to return, and they thought that your presence would not bother them on the day they needed to retrieve all their papers. But they did not count on my husband, who, on the night of June 22 to 23, forced the safe, took... what he was looking for, and left his card to clearly show the two brothers that he no longer had to fear them and that the roles had changed. Two days later, alerted by an article in Gil Blas, Étienne Varin hurried to your place, remained alone in this living room, found the safe empty... and killed himself.

After a moment, Daspry asked:

—That's just a mere assumption, isn't it? Mr. Andermatt didn't tell you anything?

—No.

—His attitude towards you hasn't changed? Did he seem darker, more troubled?

—No.

—And you believe it would be the same if he had found the letters! To me, he hasn't. To me, it's not him who entered here.

—But who then?

—The mysterious figure who is orchestrating this affair, who holds all the strings, and who is directing it toward a goal that we can only glimpse through so many complications, the mysterious figure whose visible and all-powerful influence has been felt since the very first hour. It is he and his associates who entered this hotel on June 22, it is he who discovered the hiding place, it is he who left Mr. Andermatt's card, it is he who holds the correspondence and the evidence of the Varin brothers' betrayal.

—Who, him? I interrupted, not without impatience.

—The correspondent for L'Écho de France, good heavens, that Salvator! Isn't it glaringly obvious? Doesn't he provide details in his article that only someone who has uncovered the secrets of the two brothers could know?

—In that case, stammered Mme Andermatt, horrified, he has my letters too, and now he's threatening my husband! What should I do, my God!

—Write to him, declared Daspry clearly, confide in him openly; tell him everything you know and everything you can discover.

—What are you saying!

—Your interest aligns with his. There's no doubt he is acting against the surviving brother. He isn't seeking weapons against Mr. Andermatt, but against Alfred Varin. Help him.

—How?

—Does your husband have that document that completes and allows for the use of Louis Lacombe's plans?

—Yes.

—Inform Salvator about it. If necessary, try to provide him with this document. In short, start corresponding with him. What do you have to lose?

The advice was bold, even dangerous at first glance, but Mme Andermatt had little choice. After all, as Daspry said, what did she have to lose? If the unknown person was an enemy, this action wouldn't worsen the situation. If it was a stranger pursuing a specific goal, he would likely attach only secondary importance to those letters.

In any case, it was an idea, and Mme Andermatt, in her distress, was more than happy to embrace it. She thanked us warmly and promised to keep us updated.

The day after tomorrow, indeed, she sent us this note she received in response:

"The letters were not there. But I will get them, don't worry. I'm keeping an eye on everything. S."

I took the paper. It was the writing from the note that had been slipped into my bedside book on the evening of June 22.

Daspry was indeed right; Salvator was the mastermind behind this affair.

* * *

In truth, we were beginning to see some glimmers of light amid the darkness that surrounded us, and certain points were illuminated in unexpected ways. Yet many others remained obscure, like the discovery of the two seven of hearts! For my part, I kept returning to that, perhaps more intrigued than I should have been by these two cards, whose seven tiny pierced figures had caught my eye in such troubling circumstances. What role did they play in the drama? What significance should we attribute to them? What conclusion could we draw from the fact that the submarine built according to Louis Lacombe's plans was named the Seven of Hearts?

Daspry, on the other hand, paid little attention to the two cards, fully focused on studying another problem that seemed more urgent to him: he was tirelessly searching for the famous hiding place.

—And who knows, he said, if I might not find the letters that Salvator did not find... perhaps by oversight. It's hard to believe that the Varin brothers would have taken from a place they thought inaccessible the weapon whose value they knew to be immeasurable.

And he searched. The large room soon held no more secrets for him, so he extended his investigations to all the other rooms in the pavilion: he examined the inside and outside, he scrutinized the stones and bricks of the walls, he lifted the roof slates.

One day, he arrived with a pickaxe and a shovel, handed me the shovel, kept the pickaxe, and pointing to the vacant lot, said:

—Let's go.

I followed him without enthusiasm. He divided the area into several sections, which he inspected one after the other. But in a corner, at the angle formed by the walls of two neighboring properties, a pile of stones and pebbles, covered with brambles and grass, caught his attention. He set to work on it.

I had to help him. For an hour, in the blazing sun, we toiled in vain. But when, beneath the stones we had moved aside, we reached the ground itself and had dug it up, Daspry's pickaxe exposed skeletal remains, a portion of a skeleton around which still clung tattered pieces of clothing.

And suddenly I felt myself go pale. I saw a small iron plate embedded in the ground, cut into a rectangular shape, and I thought I could make out some red stains on it. I bent down. It was indeed that: the plate was the size of a playing card, and the red stains, a faded red lead color in places, numbered seven, arranged like the seven spots on a seven of hearts, with a hole drilled at each of the seven ends.

"Listen, Daspry, I've had enough of all these stories. Good for you if you find them interesting. I'm leaving you."

Was it the emotion? Was it the fatigue from working under the harsh sun? Whatever the reason, I staggered as I left and had to go to bed, where I remained for forty-eight hours, feverish and burning, haunted by skeletons dancing around me and throwing their bloody hearts at each other.

Daspry remained loyal to me. Every day he devoted three or four hours to it, which, to be fair, he spent in the large room, rummaging, banging, and tapping.

"The letters are here, in this room," he would tell me from time to time, "they're here. I would stake my life on it."

"Leave me in peace," I replied, exasperated.

On the morning of the third day, I got up feeling still quite weak, but healed. A hearty breakfast comforted me. However, a note I received around five o'clock contributed, more than anything, to my complete recovery, as my curiosity was once again, despite everything, piqued.

The note contained these words:

"Sir,

"The drama whose first act took place on the night of June 22 to 23 is nearing its conclusion. The very nature of events requires that I bring together the two main characters of this drama, and that this confrontation takes place at your home. I would be immensely grateful if you could lend me your residence for this evening. It would be advisable for your servant to be away from nine to eleven o'clock, and it would be preferable for you to have the extreme kindness to leave the field clear for the adversaries. You may have noticed on the night of June 22 to 23 that I was scrupulous in respecting everything that belongs to you. For my part, I would consider it an affront if I doubted your absolute discretion regarding the one who signs

"Yours sincerely,

"SALVATOR."

There was a tone of courteous irony in this letter, and in the request it expressed, such a delightful whimsy that I took pleasure in it. It was charmingly casual, and my correspondent seemed so sure of my agreement! For nothing in the world would I want to disappoint him or respond to his trust with ingratitude.

At eight o'clock, my servant, to whom I had offered a theater seat, had just left when Daspry arrived. I showed him the note.

"Well?" he said to me.

—Well, I'm leaving the garden gate open so that anyone can come in.

—And are you leaving?

—Not a chance!

—But since you're being asked…

—I'm being asked to be discreet. I'll be discreet. But I'm fiercely determined to see what's going to happen.

Daspry began to laugh.

—Well, you're right, and I'm staying too. I have a feeling we won't be bored.

A bell rang, interrupting him.

—Them already? he murmured, and twenty minutes early! Impossible.

From the hallway, I pulled the cord that opened the gate. A woman's silhouette crossed the garden: Mme Andermatt.

She looked distraught and gasped as she stammered:

—My husband… he's coming… he has an appointment… we have to give him the letters…

—How do you know this? I asked her.

—By chance. A message my husband received during dinner.

—A little blue slip?

—A telephone message. The servant mistakenly handed it to me. My husband took it right away, but it was too late… I had read it.

—You had read…

—Something like this: "At nine o'clock this evening, be at Boulevard Maillot with the documents related to the case. In exchange, the letters." After dinner, I went back to my room and left.

—Without Mr. Andermatt knowing?

—Yes.

Daspry looked at me.

—What do you think?

—I think what you think, that Mr. Andermatt is one of the summoned opponents.

—By whom? And for what purpose?

—That's exactly what we're about to find out.

I led them into the large room.

We could just barely fit all three of us under the mantel of the fireplace and hide behind the velvet curtain. We settled in. Mme Andermatt sat between us. Through the slits in the curtain, the whole room was visible to us.

Nine o'clock struck. A few minutes later, the garden gate creaked on its hinges.

I must admit that I was feeling a certain anxiety and that a new excitement was overwhelming me. I was on the verge of uncovering the solution to the mystery! The perplexing adventure whose twists and turns had unfolded before me for weeks was finally about to reveal its true meaning, and the battle was about to take place right before my eyes.

Daspry took Mme Andermatt's hand and whispered:

—Above all, not a movement! Whatever you hear or see, remain still.

Someone entered. I immediately recognized, by his strong resemblance to Étienne Varin, his brother Alfred. The same heavy gait, the same earthy face overtaken by a beard.

He entered with the anxious demeanor of a man who is accustomed to fearing traps around him, who senses them and avoids them. With a quick glance, he surveyed the room, and I had the impression that the chimney concealed by a velvet curtain was unpleasant to him. He took three steps toward us. But a more pressing thought evidently diverted him, as he turned toward the wall, stopped in front of the old mosaic king, with his flowery beard and flaming sword, and examined it intently, climbing onto a chair, tracing the outline of the shoulders and face with his finger, and feeling certain parts of the image.

But suddenly, he jumped off his chair and moved away from the wall. The sound of footsteps echoed. M. Andermatt appeared in the doorway.

The banker let out a cry of surprise.

—You! You! It's you who called me?

—Me? Not at all, Varin protested in a hoarse voice that reminded me of his brother's, it was your letter that brought me here.

—My letter!

—A letter signed by you, in which you offer me...

—I haven't written to you.

—You haven't written to me!

Instinctively, Varin braced himself, not against the banker, but against the unknown enemy who had lured him into this trap. For the second time, his eyes turned towards us, and quickly, he headed for the door.

Mr. Andermatt blocked his way.

—What are you doing, Varin?

—There are machines down there that I don't like. I'm leaving. Good evening.

—Just a moment!

—Come on, Mr. Andermatt, don't insist, we have nothing to say to each other.

—We have a lot to discuss, and the opportunity is too good…

—Let me pass.

—No, no, no, you will not pass.

Varin stepped back, intimidated by the banker's resolute stance, and he muttered:

—Then, let's talk quickly, and let's get it over with!

One thing surprised me, and I was sure my two companions felt the same disappointment. How could it be that Salvator was not there? Wasn't it part of his plans to intervene? Did he really think that just the confrontation between the banker and Varin would be enough? I was particularly troubled. Due to his absence, this duel, orchestrated by him, desired by him, took on a tragic aspect akin to events that are sparked and commanded by the strict order of fate, and the force that pitted these two men against each other was all the more striking because it resided outside of them.

After a moment, Mr. Andermatt approached Varin and, facing him, eyes locked:

—Now that years have passed and you have nothing left to fear, answer me honestly, Varin. What have you done with Louis Lacombe?

—Now that's a question! As if I could know what has become of him!

—You know! You know! Your brother and you were always following in his footsteps, you practically lived at his place, in the very house where we are now. You were aware of all his work, all his plans. And on that last evening, Varin, when I walked Louis Lacombe to my door, I saw two figures slipping away into the shadows. I am ready to swear to that.

—And then, what will you do after you swear?

—It was your brother and you, Varin.

—Prove it.

—But the best proof is that, two days later, you yourself showed me the papers and plans you had gathered from Lacombe's briefcase, and you offered to sell them to me. How did those papers come into your possession?

—I told you, Mr. Andermatt, we found them on Louis Lacombe's very table the morning after his disappearance.

—That's not true.

—Prove it.

—Justice could have proven it.

—Why didn't you turn to justice?

—Why? Oh! why...

He fell silent, his face dark. And the other resumed:

—You see, Mr. Andermatt, if you had any certainty at all, it wouldn't have been the minor threat we made that would have stopped you...

—What threat? Those letters? Do you really think I ever believed for a moment?...

—If you didn't believe in those letters, why did you offer me a fortune to get them back? And why, since then, have you had my brother and me hunted down like animals?

—To get back plans that were important to me.

—Come now! It was for the letters. Once you had the letters, you would have turned us in. More often than I would have let go of them!

He burst into laughter, which he suddenly interrupted.

—But that's enough. No matter how many times we repeat the same words, we won't make any progress. So we will leave it at that.

—We will not leave it at that, said the banker, and since you mentioned the letters, you will not leave here until you return them to me.

—I will leave.

—No, no.

—Listen, Mr. Andermatt, I advise you...

—You will not leave.

—We'll see about that, said Varin with such a tone of rage that Mme Andermatt stifled a faint cry.

He must have heard it because he tried to force his way out. Mr. Andermatt violently pushed him back. Then I saw him slip his hand into the pocket of his jacket.

—One last time!

—The letters first.

Varin pulled out a revolver and, aiming it at Mr. Andermatt:

—Yes or no?

The banker quickly ducked.

A gunshot rang out. The weapon fell.

I was stunned. The shot had fired right next to me! It was Daspry who, with a bullet from his pistol, had knocked the weapon from Alfred Varin's hand!

Suddenly standing between the two adversaries, facing Varin, he sneered:

—You're lucky, my friend, very lucky. I was aiming for your hand, and I hit the revolver.

Both of them stared at him, motionless and bewildered. He said to the banker:

—You will excuse me, sir, for interfering in something that does not concern me. But really, you are playing your hand too clumsily. Allow me to hold the cards.

Turning to the other:

—Now it's our turn, comrade. And let's make it quick, please. The trump is hearts, and I play the seven.

And, just three inches from his nose, he pressed the iron plate marked with seven red dots against him.

I have never witnessed such upheaval. Pale, with wide eyes and features twisted in anguish, the man seemed hypnotized by the scene before him.

— Who are you? he stammered.

— I've already said, a gentleman who deals with matters that do not concern him... but who takes them very seriously.

— What do you want?

— Everything you have brought.

— I haven't brought anything.

— Yes, otherwise you wouldn't be here. You received a note this morning summoning you here for nine o'clock and instructing you to bring all the papers you had. And here you are. Where are the papers?

In Daspry's voice, in his demeanor, there was an authority that unsettled me, a way of acting completely new for this usually laid-back and gentle man. Completely subdued, Varin pointed to one of his pockets.

— The papers are there.

— Are they all there?

—Yes.

— All those you found in Louis Lacombe's briefcase and sold to Major von Lieben?

—Yes.

— Is it the copy or the original?

— The original.

— How much do you want for it?

— A hundred thousand.

Daspry laughed.

— You're crazy. The major only gave you twenty thousand. Twenty thousand wasted, since the tests failed.

— They didn't know how to use the plans.

— The plans are incomplete.

— Then why are you asking me for them?

— I need them. I'm offering you five thousand francs. Not a sou more.

— Ten thousand. Not a sou less.

— Agreed.

Daspry turned back to Mr. Andermatt.

— Please sign a check, sir.

— But... I don't have...

— Your checkbook? Here it is.

Dumbfounded, Mr. Andermatt felt the checkbook that Daspry handed him.

— It is indeed mine... How is this possible?

— No empty words, please, dear sir, just sign.

The banker took out his fountain pen and signed. Varin extended his hand.

"Keep your hands off," Daspry said, "everything isn't finished yet."

And addressing the banker:

"There was also talk of letters that you're demanding?"

"Yes, a package of letters."

"Where are they, Varin?"

"I don't have them."

"Where are they, Varin?"

"I don't know. My brother was responsible for them."

"They're hidden here, in this room."

"In that case, you know where they are."

"How would I know?"

"Well, aren't you the one who visited the hiding place? You seem as well-informed… as Salvator."

"The letters are not in the hiding place."

"They are there."

"Open it."

Varin shot a look of defiance. Were Daspry and Salvator really one and the same, as everything suggested? If so, he had nothing to lose by revealing a hiding place that was already known. If not, it would be pointless…

"Open it," Daspry repeated.

"I don't have the seven of hearts."

"Yes, that one," said Daspry, holding out the iron plate.

Varin recoiled, terrified:

"No… no… I don't want to…"

"Never mind that…"

Daspry approached the old monarch with the flowing beard, climbed onto a chair, and placed the seven of hearts at the base of the sword, against the hilt, so that the edges of the plate exactly covered both edges of the sword. Then, with the help of a punch, which he inserted alternately into each of the seven holes at the end of the seven points of hearts, he pressed down on seven of the small stones in the mosaic. At the seventh small stone pressed in, a trigger was activated, and the entire bust of the king pivoted, revealing a large opening designed like a chest, with iron linings and two gleaming steel shelves.

"You see, Varin, the chest is empty."

—Indeed... So my brother must have taken the letters.

Daspry returned to the man and said:

—Don't try to outsmart me. There's another hiding place. Where is it?

—There isn't one.

—Is it money you want? How much?

—Ten thousand.

—Mr. Andermatt, are those letters worth ten thousand francs to you?

—Yes, the banker replied in a loud voice.

Varin closed the safe, took the seven of hearts, not without visible reluctance, and placed it against the sword, right at the guard, and precisely at the same spot. He then drove the punch into each of the seven heart points. A second trigger was activated, but this time, unexpectedly, only a part of the safe pivoted, revealing a small compartment built into the thickness of the door that closed the larger safe.

The bundle of letters was there, tied with string and sealed. Varin handed it to Daspry. Daspry asked:

—Is the check ready, Mr. Andermatt?

—Yes.

—And do you also have the final document you received from Louis Lacombe, which completes the submarine plans?

—Yes.

The exchange took place. Daspry pocketed the document and the check and offered the bundle to Mr. Andermatt.

—Here is what you wanted, sir.

The banker hesitated for a moment, as if afraid to touch those cursed pages he had searched for so desperately. Then, with a nervous gesture, he took it.

Next to me, I heard a moan. I grabbed the hand of Mme Andermatt: it was cold.

And Daspry said to the banker:

—I believe, sir, that our conversation is over. Oh! No thanks, please. It was only by chance that I could be of help to you.

Mr. Andermatt left. He took with him the letters from his wife to Louis Lacombe.

—Wonderful, exclaimed Daspry with a delighted air, everything is falling into place. We just need to wrap up our business, comrade. Do you have the papers?

—Here they all are.

Daspry reviewed them, examined them carefully, and then stuffed them into his pocket.

—Perfect, you kept your word.

—But…

—But what?

—The two checks? … the money? …

—Well, you have some nerve, my friend. How dare you demand!

—I'm claiming what is owed to me.

—So, you're owed something for papers that you stole?

But the man seemed beside himself. He trembled with rage, his eyes bloodshot.

—The money ... the twenty thousand ... he stammered.

—Impossible ... I have a use for it.

—The money! ...

—Come on, be reasonable, and keep your knife to yourself.

He grabbed his arm so roughly that the other screamed in pain, and added:

—Go on, comrade, some fresh air will do you good. Do you want me to walk you out? We can go through the vacant lot, and I'll show you a pile of stones under which...

—That's not true! That's not true!

—Oh yes, it's true. That little iron plate with seven red dots came from over there. It never left Louis Lacombe, remember? You and your brother buried it with the corpse... along with other things that will greatly interest the authorities.

Varin covered his face with his furious fists. Then he said:

—Fine. I'm done for. Let's not speak of it anymore. One word, though... just one word... I would like to know...

—I'm listening.

—There was a box in that chest, in the larger of the two, a casket?

—Yes.

—When you came here, the night of June 22 to 23, was it there?

—Yes.

—What did it contain?...

—Everything that the Varin brothers had locked away, a rather nice collection of jewelry, diamonds, and pearls, was taken from right and left by those brothers.

—And you took it?

—Well! Put yourself in my shoes.

—So… it was upon realizing the disappearance of the box that my brother killed himself?

—Probably. The disappearance of your correspondence with Major von Lieben wouldn't have been enough. But the disappearance of the box… Is that all you wanted to ask me?

—One more thing: your name?

—You say that as if you have thoughts of revenge.

—Of course! Fortune changes. Today you are the strongest. Tomorrow…

—It will be you.

—I'm counting on it. Your name?

—Arsène Lupin.

—Arsène Lupin!

The man staggered, as if struck by a club. It seemed that those two words took away all his hope. Daspry began to laugh.

—Ah! Did you think that a Mr. Durand or Dupont could have pulled off such a grand affair? Come on, it required at least an Arsène Lupin. And now that you're informed, my little friend, go prepare your revenge. Arsène Lupin is waiting for you.

And he pushed him outside, without another word.

* * *

—Daspry, Daspry, I shouted, still calling him by the name under which I had known him, despite myself.

I pulled aside the velvet curtain.

He rushed over.

—What? What's going on?

—Mme Andermatt is unwell.

He hurried to her, made her breathe some salts, and while treating her, he asked me:

—Well, what happened?

—The letters, I told him... the letters from Louis Lacombe that you gave to her husband!

He struck his forehead.

—She thought I did that!... But yes, after all, she could believe it. What an idiot I am!

Mme Andermatt, revitalized, listened eagerly. He pulled out a small package from his wallet, identical to the one Mr. Andermatt had taken.

—Here are your letters, madam, the real ones.

—But... what about the others?

—The others are the same as these, but copied by me last night, and carefully arranged. Your husband will be even happier to read them since he won't suspect any substitution, as everything seemed to happen right before his eyes...

—The handwriting...

—There's no handwriting that can't be imitated.

She thanked him with the same words of gratitude she would have given to a man of her social circle, and I could tell she hadn't heard the last few exchanges between Varin and Arsène Lupin.

I looked at him, feeling somewhat embarrassed, unsure of what to say to this former friend who was revealing himself in such an unexpected light. Lupin! It was Lupin! My companion from the circle was none other than Lupin! I couldn't believe it. But he, very at ease:

—You can say goodbye to Jean Daspry.

—Oh!

—Yes, Jean Daspry is going on a trip. I'm sending him to Morocco. It's quite possible he will meet a fitting end there. I even admit that it's his intention.

—But Arsène Lupin remains with us?

—Oh! more than ever. Arsène Lupin is only at the beginning of his career, and he intends to…

An irresistible curiosity drove me to him, pulling him a little distance away from Mme Andermatt:

—So, you finally discovered the second hiding place, the one where the package of letters was?

—I had quite a bit of trouble! Just yesterday afternoon, while you were resting. And yet, God knows how easy it was! But the simplest things are often the last ones we think of.

And showing me the seven of hearts:

— I had guessed that, to open the large chest, I needed to press this card against the sword of the mosaic man…

— How did you figure that out?

— Easily. From my private information, I knew when I came here on the evening of June 22…

— After leaving me…

— Yes, and after putting you in a state of mind through carefully chosen conversations such that a nervous and impressionable person like you would inevitably let me act as I wished, without getting out of bed.

— The reasoning was sound.

— So, I knew when I arrived here that there was a hidden box in a chest with a secret lock, and that the seven of hearts was the key, the word for that lock. It was only a matter of pressing this seven of hearts in a spot that was clearly reserved for it. An hour of examination was enough for me.

— An hour!

— Observe the mosaic man.

— The old emperor?

— This old emperor is the exact representation of the king of hearts from all card games, Charlemagne.

— Indeed... But why does the seven of hearts sometimes open the large chest and sometimes the small one? And why did you first open only the large chest?

— Why? Because I was always stubbornly placing my seven of hearts in the same orientation. Just yesterday I realized that by flipping it, that is, by putting the seventh point, the one in the middle, up instead of down, the arrangement of the seven points changed.

— Good heavens!

— Obviously, good heavens, but one still had to think of it.

— Another thing: you were unaware of the story of the letters before Mme Andermatt...

—Did you speak in front of me? Yes. I had discovered in the chest, besides the cassette, only the correspondence between the two brothers, correspondence that put me on the trail of their betrayal.

—In the end, it was by chance that you were led, first to reconstruct the story of the two brothers, and then to search for the plans and documents of the submarine?

—By chance.

—But what was your purpose in searching?...

Daspry interrupted me with a laugh:

—My God! how interesting this case is to you!

—It fascinates me.

—Well, just now, when I have seen Mme Andermatt off and sent the message I'm about to write to the Écho de France, I will return and we will get into the details.

He sat down and wrote one of those brief notes that reflected the character's whimsy. Who doesn't remember the stir it caused around the world?

"Arsène Lupin has solved the problem posed by Salvator recently. Having control of all the original documents and plans of engineer Louis Lacombe, he has sent them to the Minister of the Navy. On this occasion, he is starting a subscription to offer the State the first submarine constructed based on these plans. He himself is subscribing at the top of this list for the sum of twenty thousand francs."

—The twenty thousand francs from Mr. Andermatt's checks? I asked him after he handed me the paper to read.

—Exactly. It was only fair that Varin partially redeemed his betrayal.

* * *

And that's how I came to know Arsène Lupin. That's how I discovered that Jean Daspry, my companion from the circle, a social acquaintance, was none other than Arsène Lupin, the gentleman burglar. That's how I forged a pleasant friendship with our great man, and how, gradually, thanks to the trust he graciously bestows upon me, I became his very humble, very loyal, and very grateful historian.

CHAPTER SEVEN
THE SAFE OF MADAME IMBERT

At three in the morning, there were still half a dozen carriages in front of one of the small painter's hotels that line the only side of the Boulevard Berthier. The door of this hotel opened. A group of guests, both men and women, emerged. Four carriages whisked away in different directions, leaving only two gentlemen who parted ways at the corner of Rue de Courcelles, where one of them lived. The other decided to walk back to Porte-Maillot.

He crossed Avenue de Villiers and continued along the sidewalk opposite the fortifications. On this beautiful winter night, clear and cold, it was a pleasure to walk. The air was refreshing, and the sound of footsteps echoed cheerfully.

But after a few minutes, he had the uncomfortable feeling that someone was following him. Indeed, when he turned around, he spotted the shadow of a man slipping between the trees. He was not easily frightened; however, he quickened his pace to reach the Ternes toll gate as soon as possible. But the man began to run. Feeling quite uneasy, he deemed it wiser to confront him and drew his revolver from his pocket.

He didn't have time. The man attacked him violently, and immediately a struggle began on the deserted boulevard, a grappling fight where he quickly realized he was at a disadvantage. He called for help, struggled, and was thrown against a pile of stones, his throat gripped, a handkerchief stuffed into his mouth by his assailant. His eyes closed, his ears buzzed, and he was on the verge of losing consciousness when suddenly, the grip loosened, and the man who had been suffocating him got up to defend himself against an unexpected attack.

A strike of a cane on the wrist, a kick to the ankle... the man let out two groans of pain and fled, limping and swearing.

Without bothering to pursue him, the newcomer leaned down and said:

—Are you hurt, sir?

He wasn't hurt, but he was quite dazed and unable to stand. Fortunately, one of the customs officers, drawn by the screams, rushed over. A carriage was summoned. The gentleman took a seat alongside his savior, and they were taken to his hotel on the Avenue de la Grande-Armée.

At the door, fully recovered, he expressed his gratitude profusely.

—I owe you my life, sir; please believe that I will not forget it. I don't want to frighten my wife right now, but I want her to express my gratitude to you herself as soon as possible.

He invited him to lunch and told him his name: Ludovic Imbert, adding:

—May I know to whom I have the honor of speaking...

—Of course, replied the other.

And he introduced himself:

—Arsène Lupin.

* * *

Arsène Lupin didn't have the fame that would come from the Cahorn case, his escape from La Santé prison, and many other sensational exploits. In fact, he wasn't even called Arsène Lupin at that time. This name, which would later shine so brightly in the future, was specifically created to identify the savior of Mr. Imbert, and it can be said that it was in this case that he received his baptism by fire. Ready for battle, it is true, equipped in every way, but without resources or the authority that success brings, Arsène Lupin was merely an apprentice in a profession where he would soon become a master.

So what a thrill of joy he felt upon waking, when he remembered the invitation from the night before! Finally, he was close to his goal! Finally, he was embarking on a task worthy of his strength and talent! The millions of the Imberts—what a magnificent prize for an appetite like his!

He made a special effort with his attire: a worn frock coat, frayed trousers, a slightly reddish silk hat, tattered cuffs and collar, all quite clean but smelling of poverty. For a tie, he wore a black ribbon pinned with a surprise nut diamond. And dressed like this, he descended the stairs of the apartment he occupied in Montmartre. On the third floor, without stopping, he tapped the pommel of his cane on the panel of a closed door. Outside, he made his way to the outer boulevards. A tram passed by. He took a seat, and someone walking behind him, the tenant of the third floor, sat down beside him.

After a moment, the man said to him:

—So, boss?

—Well, it's done.

—How?

—I'm having lunch there.

—You're having lunch there!

—I hope you wouldn't want me to have wasted such precious days of mine for nothing? I pulled Mr. Ludovic Imbert from the certain death you had planned for him. Mr. Ludovic Imbert is a grateful man. He has invited me to lunch.

There was a silence, and the other ventured:

—So, you're not giving up?

—My dear, Arsène replied, if I orchestrated the little incident last night, if I took the trouble, at three in the morning, along the fortifications, to give you a whack on the wrist with my cane and a kick on the shin, risking injury to my only friend, it's not to back down now from the benefits of a rescue so well planned.

—But the bad rumors circulating about the fortune…

—Let them circulate. I've been pursuing this matter for six months, six months during which I've gathered information, studied, set my traps, questioned servants, lenders, and front men, six months living in the shadows of the husband and wife. Therefore, I know what to expect. Whether the fortune comes from old Brawford, as they claim, or from another source, I affirm that it exists. And since it exists, it is mine.

—Goodness, a hundred million!

—Let's say ten, or even five, it doesn't matter! There are large bundles of securities in the safe. It would be quite the devil if, sooner or later, I don't get my hands on the key.

The tramway stopped at the Place de l'Étoile. The man murmured:

—So, for the moment?

—For the moment, nothing to be done. I'll let you know. We have time.

Five minutes later, Arsène Lupin was ascending the sumptuous staircase of the Imbert hotel, and Ludovic was introducing him to his wife. Gervaise was a lovely little lady, round and very talkative. She gave Lupin a warm welcome.

"I wanted us to celebrate our savior alone," she said.

And right from the start, "our savior" was treated like an old friend. By dessert, the intimacy was complete, and confidences flowed freely. Arsène recounted his life, the life of his father, an upright magistrate, the sorrows of his childhood, and the challenges he faced in the present. Gervaise, in turn, shared her youth, her marriage, the kindness of the old Brawford, the hundred million she had inherited, the obstacles delaying her access to it, the loans she had to take out at exorbitant rates, her endless disputes with Brawford's nephews, and the legal challenges! And the seizures! Everything, in fact!

"Just think, Mr. Lupin, the titles are right there, next door, in my husband's office, and if we detach even one coupon, we lose everything! They are in our safe, and we can't touch them!"

A slight shiver ran through Mr. Lupin at the thought of that proximity. He had a very clear sensation that Mr. Lupin would never have the moral elevation to feel the same scruples as the good lady.

"Ah, they are there," he murmured, his throat dry.

"They are there."

Relationships that began under such auspices could only grow tighter. When gently questioned, Arsène Lupin confessed his misery, his distress. Immediately, the unfortunate young man was appointed the private secretary to the couple, with a salary of one hundred fifty francs per month. He would continue living in his own place, but would come every day to take work orders, and for convenience, a room on the second floor was made available to him as an office.

He chose. What a fortunate coincidence that it was located above Ludovic's office!

* * *

Arsène quickly realized that his position as secretary resembled a cushy job. In two months, he only had four insignificant letters to copy and was called into his boss's office just once, which allowed him the opportunity to officially gaze at the safe. Furthermore, he noted that the holder of this cushy job did not seem worthy of being included alongside Deputy Anquety or the bar association president Grouvel, as he was excluded from the famous social receptions.

He did not complain, preferring to keep his modest little position in the shadows and stayed away, happy and free. Besides, he wasn't wasting his time. He first made a number of covert visits to Ludovic's office and paid his respects to the safe, which remained firmly locked. It was a massive block of cast iron and steel, with a forbidding appearance, against which neither files, nor drills, nor any other tools could prevail.

Arsène Lupin was not stubborn.

—Where brute force fails, cunning succeeds, he thought. The key is to have an eye and an ear in the place.

He therefore took the necessary measures, and after meticulous and painstaking probing through the floor of his room, he installed a lead pipe that led to the ceiling of the office between two moldings of the cornice. Through this pipe, serving as an acoustic tube and a viewing device, he hoped to see and hear.

From then on, he lived flat on his stomach on the floorboards. Indeed, he often saw the Imberts holding meetings in front of the safe, poring over ledgers and handling files. When they successively turned the four buttons that controlled the lock, he tried to count the clicks to know the combination. He watched their movements and listened closely to their words. What were they doing with the key? Were they hiding it?

One day, he hurried downstairs when he saw them leaving the room without closing the safe. He resolutely entered. They had returned.

—Oh! Excuse me, he said, I must have come to the wrong door.

But Gervaise rushed forward and pulled him in:

—Come in, Mr. Lupin, come in, aren't you at home here? You're going to give us some advice. Which securities should we sell? The External ones or the Rente?

—But what about the opposition? Lupin objected, quite surprised.

—Oh! It doesn't affect all the securities.

She pushed the door open. On the shelves, portfolios strapped with bands were piled up. She grabbed one. But her husband protested.

—No, no, Gervaise, it would be crazy to sell the External ones. They're going to go up… While the Rente is at its peak. What do you think, my dear friend?

The dear friend had no opinion, yet he advised sacrificing the Rente. So she took another bundle and, at random, pulled out a piece of paper. It was a 3% bond worth 1,374 francs. Ludovic slipped it into his pocket. That afternoon, accompanied by his secretary, he had the bond sold by a stockbroker and collected forty-six thousand francs.

Whatever Gervaise might have said, Arsène Lupin did not feel at home. On the contrary, his situation at the Imbert hotel filled him with surprise. On several occasions, he noticed that the servants were unaware of his name. They called him "sir." Ludovic always referred to him this way: "You will inform sir… Has sir arrived?" Why this enigmatic title?

Moreover, after the initial enthusiasm, the Imberts barely spoke to him, and while treating him with the respect due to a benefactor, they never concerned themselves with him! They seemed to regard him as an eccentric who preferred not to be bothered, and they respected his solitude as though it were a rule set by him, a whim of his own. Once, as he passed through the vestibule, he overheard Gervaise saying to two gentlemen:

"He's such a savage!"

Fine, he thought, we are savages. And giving up on trying to understand the oddities of these people, he continued to carry out his plan. He was convinced that he could not rely on chance or on Gervaise's carelessness, as the key to the safe did not leave her side, and besides, she would never have taken that key without first jamming the lock's letters. Therefore, he had to take action.

An event hastened things along: the intense campaign waged against the Imberts by certain newspapers. They were accused of fraud. Arsène Lupin witnessed the unfolding drama, the couple's agitation, and he realized that if he delayed any longer, he would lose everything.

For five consecutive days, instead of leaving around six o'clock as he usually did, he locked himself in his room. They assumed he had gone out. He lay on the floor and kept an eye on Ludovic's office.

For five evenings, the favorable circumstance he had been waiting for had not occurred, so he left in the middle of the night through the small door that led to the courtyard. He had a key for it.

But on the sixth day, he learned that the Imberts, in response to the malicious insinuations of their enemies, had proposed to open the chest and take inventory of its contents.

"Tonight is the night," thought Lupin.

And indeed, after dinner, Ludovic settled into his office. Gervaise joined him. They began to leaf through the records of the chest.

An hour passed, then another hour. He heard the servants going to bed. Now there was no one left on the first floor. Midnight. The Imberts continued their work.

"Let's go," murmured Lupin.

He opened his window. It faced the courtyard, and the space, under the moonless and starless night, was dark. He pulled a knotted rope from his wardrobe, secured it to the balcony railing, swung over, and let himself slide down gently, using a downspout, until he reached the window below his own. It was the office window, and the thick curtain drapes concealed the room. Standing on the balcony, he paused for a moment, listening intently and keeping a watchful eye.

Reassured by the silence, he gently pushed open the two casements. If no one had bothered to check them, they should yield to his effort, as he had turned the latch earlier in the afternoon so that it no longer engaged the catches.

The casements opened. Then, with infinite caution, he pushed them open further. As soon as he could slip his head through, he stopped. A bit of light filtered between the two misaligned curtains: he spotted Gervaise and Ludovic sitting next to the chest.

They exchanged only a few quiet words, absorbed in their work. Arsène calculated the distance that separated him from them, determined the exact movements he would need to make to incapacitate them one by one, before they had time to call for help, and he was about to spring into action when Gervaise said:

—It's gotten quite cold in here since a moment ago! I'm going to bed. And you?

—I'd like to finish.

—Finish! But it'll take you all night.

—No, just an hour at most.

She left. Twenty minutes, thirty minutes passed. Arsène pushed the window open a bit more. The curtains fluttered. He pushed again. Ludovic turned around, and seeing the curtains billowing in the wind, got up to close the window...

There was not a single scream, not even a hint of a struggle. In a few precise movements, and without causing him any harm, Arsène stunned him, wrapped his head with the curtain, tied him up, in such a way that Ludovic could not even see the face of his attacker.

Then, quickly, he headed towards the safe, grabbed two wallets and tucked them under his arm, left the office, went down the stairs, crossed the courtyard, and opened the service door. A carriage was waiting in the street.

—Take this first, he said to the driver, and follow me.

He returned to the office. In two trips, they emptied the safe. Then Arsène went up to his room, removed the rope, and erased any trace of his passage. It was done.

A few hours later, Arsène Lupin, assisted by his companion, proceeded to examine the contents of the wallets. He felt no disappointment, having anticipated it, upon realizing that the Imbert family's fortune was not as significant as it had been made out to be. The millions were not counted in hundreds, nor even in tens. But still, the total formed a very respectable figure, consisting of excellent assets: railway bonds, Paris city bonds, state funds, Suez, northern mines, etc.

He declared himself satisfied.

—Certainly, he said, there will be a tough loss when the time comes to negotiate. We will face opposition, and more than once we will have to liquidate at a low price. Nevertheless, with this initial investment, I'll manage to live as I please... and to fulfill a few dreams that are dear to me.

—And the rest?

—You can burn it, my dear. Those piles of papers looked good in the safe. For us, they are useless. As for the securities, we will quietly lock them away in the cupboard, and wait for the right moment.

The next day, Arsène thought that nothing prevented him from returning to the Imbert hotel. But reading the newspapers revealed the unexpected news: Ludovic and Gervaise had disappeared.

The opening of the safe took place with great solemnity. The magistrates found what Arsène Lupin had left behind... very little.

* * *

Such are the facts, and such is the explanation that Arsène Lupin gives for certain of them. I heard the account directly from him one day when he was in a mood to confide.

That day, he was pacing back and forth in my study, and there was a slight feverish gleam in his eyes that I had never seen before.

—All in all, I said to him, is this your greatest heist?

Without answering me directly, he continued:

—There are impenetrable secrets in this matter. Even after the explanation I gave you, how many obscurities remain! Why this flight? Why didn't they take advantage of the help I was unintentionally offering them? It would have been so simple to say: "The one hundred million were in the safe. They are no longer there because they were stolen!"

—They lost their heads.

—Yes, that's it, they lost their heads... On the other hand, it is true...

—It is true?...

—No, nothing.

What did this hesitation mean? He hadn't said everything; it was obvious, and what he hadn't said he was reluctant to reveal. I was intrigued. It must have been serious to cause hesitation in such a man.

I asked him random questions.

—You haven't seen them again?

—No.

—And you haven't felt any pity for those two unfortunate souls?

—Me! he exclaimed, startled.

His outrage surprised me. Had I hit a nerve? I pressed on:

—Of course. Without you, they might have been able to face the danger... or at least leave with their pockets full.

—Remorse, that's what you're attributing to me, isn't it?

—Well!

He slammed his hand down on my table.

—So, according to you, I should feel remorse?

—Call it remorse or regret, in short, some kind of feeling...

—Some kind of feeling for people...

—For people from whom you stole a fortune.

—What fortune?

—Well... those two or three bundles of securities...

—Those two or three bundles of securities! I stole a few packets of securities from them, didn't I? A part of their inheritance? That's my fault? That's my crime?

"But, for heaven's sake, my dear, didn't you guess that those securities were fake?... Do you understand?

CHAPTER EIGHT
THEY WERE WRONG!

I looked at him, stunned.

—Wrong, the four or five million.

—Wrong, he shouted furiously, completely wrong! The bonds, the City of Paris, government funds, just paper, nothing but paper! Not a penny, I didn't pull a penny from the whole block! And you ask me to feel remorse? But they should be the ones feeling it! They swindled me like a common fool! They plucked me like their last duped mark, the most foolish one!

A genuine anger shook him, fueled by resentment and wounded pride.

—But from start to finish, I was on the losing end! From the very first hour! Do you know the role I played in this affair, or rather the role they made me play? The role of André Brawford! Yes, my dear, and I was completely taken in!

"It was only later, through the newspapers and by piecing together certain details, that I realized. While I was posing as the benefactor, the gentleman who risked his life to save you from the clutches of the thugs, they were making me pass off as one of the Brawfords!

"Isn't it remarkable? That character who had his room on the second floor, that savage they pointed out from a distance, that was Brawford, and Brawford was me! And thanks to me, thanks to the trust I inspired under the name of Brawford, the bankers were lending, and the notaries were urging their clients to lend! Huh, what a school for a beginner! Ah! I swear that lesson has served me well!

He stopped abruptly, grabbed my arm, and in an exasperated tone, which nonetheless revealed hints of irony and admiration, he said to me this unforgettable phrase:

—My dear, at this moment, Gervaise Imbert owes me fifteen hundred francs!

For the occasion, I couldn't help but laugh. It was truly a superior kind of buffoonery. And he himself burst into genuine merriment.

—Yes, my dear, fifteen hundred francs! Not only have I not received a single sou of my salary, but she also borrowed fifteen hundred francs from me! All my savings from my youth! And do you know why? I'll give you a hint... For her poor! Just as I said! For supposed unfortunate souls she was helping without Ludovic's knowledge!

"And I cut into that! Isn't it funny, huh? Arsène Lupin is back with fifteen hundred francs, and it's from the good lady from whom he stole four million in fake securities! And how many combinations, efforts, and brilliant tricks I had to come up with to achieve such a fine result!

"It's the only time I've been taken in my life. But by thunder, I was well and truly taken that time, and in grand style!...

CHAPTER NINE
THE BLACK PEARL

A loud ring at the doorbell woke the concierge of number 9 on Avenue Hoche. She pulled the cord while grumbling:

—I thought everyone was back. It's at least three o'clock!

Her husband muttered:

—Maybe it's for the doctor.

Indeed, a voice asked:

—Dr. Harel... what floor?

—Third on the left. But the doctor doesn't make house calls at night.

—He'll have to make one.

The man entered the hallway, climbed one floor, two floors, and without even stopping at Dr. Harel's landing, continued up to the fifth. There, he tried two keys. One worked the lock, the other the security bolt.

"Wonderful," he murmured, "the task is considerably simplified. But before taking action, we need to secure our escape. Let's see... have I logically had enough time to ring the doctor and be dismissed by him? Not yet... just a little more patience..."

After about ten minutes, he went back downstairs and bumped against the window of the lodge, grumbling about the doctor. They opened the door for him, and he slammed it shut behind him. However, this door did not close properly, as the man had quickly placed a piece of metal on the latch to prevent the bolt from engaging.

He then quietly re-entered, unnoticed by the concierges. In case of alarm, his retreat was assured.

Calmly, he climbed the five flights of stairs. In the anteroom, illuminated by an electric lantern, he placed his overcoat and hat on one of the chairs, sat down on another, and wrapped his boots in thick felt slippers.

"Phew! That's done... and how easy it was! I wonder why everyone doesn't choose the comfortable profession of burglar? With a bit of skill and thought, there's nothing more delightful. A perfectly relaxing job... a job for a family man... Too convenient, really... it becomes tedious."

He unfolded a detailed map of the apartment.

"Let's start by getting oriented. Here, I see the rectangle of the vestibule where I am. On the street side, the living room, the boudoir, and the dining room. No need to waste time there; it seems the countess has terrible taste... not a single valuable trinket!... So, straight to the point... Ah! Here's the layout of a corridor, the corridor that leads to the bedrooms. In three meters, I should encounter the door to the wardrobe that connects to the countess's bedroom."

He folded up his plan, extinguished his lantern, and ventured into the hallway while counting:

—One meter... Two meters... three meters... Here's the door... How everything aligns, my God! A simple lock, a little lock, separates me from the room, and, what's more, I know that this lock is positioned one meter forty-three from the floor... So, with a slight incision that I will make around it, we'll be rid of it...

He took the necessary tools from his pocket, but an idea stopped him.

—And what if, by chance, this lock isn't engaged? Let's try anyway... For what it costs!

He turned the doorknob. The door opened.

—My good Lupin, luck is truly on your side. What do you need now? You know the layout of the place where you're about to operate; you know where the countess hides the black pearl... Therefore, to claim the black pearl as yours, it's simply a matter of being quieter than silence, more invisible than night.

Arsène Lupin took about half an hour to open the second door, a glass door leading to the bedroom. But he did it with such care that even if the countess had not been asleep, no suspicious creaking would have disturbed her.

According to his plan, he only had to follow the outline of a chaise longue. This led him to an armchair, then to a small table near the bed. On the table, there was a box of stationery, and simply enclosed in this box was the black pearl.

He lay down on the carpet and traced the contours of the chaise longue. But at the end, he stopped to suppress the pounding of his heart. Although no fear stirred within him, he found it impossible to overcome that kind of nervous anxiety one feels in overwhelming silence. He was surprised by this, as he had lived through moments far more solemn without any emotional response. No danger threatened him. So why was his heart racing like a frenzied bell? Was it the sight of that sleeping woman that affected him, this life so close to his own?

He listened and thought he could discern the rhythm of a breath. He felt reassured, as if by a friendly presence.

He searched for the chair, then, with small, cautious movements, crawled towards the table, feeling for the shadow of his outstretched arm. His right hand encountered one of the table legs.

Finally! He just had to get up, grab the pearl, and leave. Thank goodness! for his heart was starting to race in his chest like a terrified beast, making such noise that it seemed impossible the countess wouldn't wake.

He calmed it with an extraordinary burst of willpower, but at the moment he tried to rise, his left hand hit something on the carpet, an object he immediately recognized as a candlestick, a knocked-over candlestick; and right after, another object came into view, a clock, one of those small travel clocks covered in leather.

What? What was happening? He didn't understand. This candlestick... this clock... why weren't these objects in their usual places? Ah! What was going on in the frightening darkness?

And suddenly, a cry escaped him. He had touched... oh! what a strange, indescribable thing! But no, no, fear clouded his mind. For twenty seconds, thirty seconds, he stood frozen, terrified, sweat at his temples. And his fingers retained the sensation of that contact.

With relentless effort, he reached out his arm again. His hand once more brushed against the thing, the strange, indescribable thing. He felt it. He demanded that his hand explore it and make sense of it. It was hair, a face... and that face was cold, almost icy.

As terrifying as reality may be, a man like Arsène Lupin masters it as soon as he becomes aware of it. Quickly, he activated the spring of his lantern. A woman lay before him, covered in blood. Horrible wounds devastated her neck and shoulders. He leaned down and examined her. She was dead.

—Dead, dead, he repeated in shock.

And he looked at those unblinking eyes, the grimace of that mouth, that livid flesh, and the blood, all that blood that had flowed onto the carpet and was now congealing, thick and black.

Rising, he turned on the electricity, and the room filled with light, allowing him to see all the signs of a fierce struggle. The bed was completely disheveled, the blankets and sheets torn apart. On the floor, the candlestick, then the clock—the hands marked eleven twenty—then further away, an overturned chair, and everywhere blood, puddles of blood.

—And the black pearl? he murmured.

The stationery box was in its place. He opened it quickly. It contained the case. But the case was empty.

"Goodness," he said to himself, "you boasted a bit too soon about your luck, my friend Arsène Lupin… The countess is dead, the black pearl is missing… the situation isn't looking good! We should get out of here, or you might end up facing serious consequences."

Yet he did not move.

"Get out? Yes, someone else would. But Arsène Lupin? Surely there's something better to do? Let's take this step by step. After all, your conscience is clear… Imagine you are a police commissioner and you have to conduct an investigation… Yes, but for that, one would need a clearer mind. And mine is in disarray!"

He collapsed into an armchair, his fists pressed against his burning forehead.

* * *

The case on Avenue Hoche is one of those that has intrigued us the most in recent times, and I certainly would not have recounted it if Arsène Lupin's involvement did not cast it in a particularly intriguing light. Few suspect his participation. In any case, no one knows the exact and curious truth.

Who did not know, having met her in the Bois, Léontine Zalti, the former singer, wife and widow of Count d'Andillot, the Zalti whose luxury dazzled Paris some twenty years ago, the Zalti, Countess d'Andillot, whose diamond and pearl adornments earned her a European reputation? It was said that she bore on her shoulders the fortune of several banks and the gold mines of several Australian companies. The great jewelers worked for the Zalti as they once worked for kings and queens.

And who does not remember the catastrophe where all these riches were swallowed up? Bank houses and gold mines, the abyss devoured everything. From the marvelous collection, scattered by the auctioneer, only the famous black pearl remained. The black pearl! That is to say, a fortune, if she had wanted to part with it.

She did not want to. She preferred to live modestly in a simple apartment with her lady's maid, her cook, and a servant, rather than sell this priceless jewel. There was a reason for this that she did not hesitate to confess: the black pearl was a gift from an emperor! And almost ruined, reduced to the most modest existence, she remained loyal to her companion from better days.

"As long as I live," she said, "I will not part with it."

From morning till night, she wore it around her neck. At night, she kept it in a place known only to her.

All these facts recalled by the public papers stirred curiosity, and, strangely enough but easy to understand for those who have the key to the riddle, it was precisely the arrest of the presumed assassin that complicated the mystery and prolonged the excitement. The day after, in fact, the newspapers published the following news:

"We have been informed of the arrest of Victor Danègre, the servant of Countess d'Andillot. The evidence against him is overwhelming. On the satin sleeve of his livery jacket, which Mr. Dudouis, the chief of security, found in his attic, between the bed frame and the mattress, bloodstains were discovered. Moreover, a button covered with fabric was missing from this jacket. This button had been picked up from under the victim's bed at the very start of the searches."

"It is likely that after dinner, Danègre, instead of returning to his attic, slipped into the dressing room, and from the glass door, he saw the countess hide the black pearl.

"We must say that, so far, no evidence has come to confirm this assumption. In any case, another point remains unclear. At seven in the morning, Danègre went to the tobacco shop on Boulevard de Courcelles: first the concierge, then the shopkeeper testified to this effect. On the other hand, the countess's cook and her lady's maid, who both sleep at the end of the hallway, assert that at eight o'clock, when they got up, the door to the anteroom and the kitchen door were locked tight. Having served the countess for twenty years, these two women are above all suspicion. Therefore, one wonders how Danègre could have left the apartment. Did he have another key made? The investigation will clarify these different points."

The investigation did not clarify anything at all; on the contrary, it revealed that Victor Danègre was a dangerous repeat offender, an alcoholic, and a debauchee, who was not deterred by a knife wound. However, as the case was studied further, it seemed to become shrouded in thicker darkness and more inexplicable contradictions.

First, a Miss de Sinclèves, cousin and sole heiress of the victim, stated that the countess, a month before her death, had confided to her in one of her letters how she hid the black pearl. The day after she received this letter, she noticed it was missing. Who had stolen it?"

On their part, the concierges reported that they had opened the door for an individual who then went upstairs to Dr. Harel's place. The doctor was summoned. No one had rung his doorbell. So who was this individual? An accomplice?

This theory of an accomplice was adopted by the press and the public. Ganimard, the old chief inspector, defended it, not without reason.

—There's some Lupin behind this, he told the judge.

—Oh! the judge replied, you see Lupin everywhere.

—I see him everywhere because he is everywhere.

—You should say you see him whenever something doesn't seem quite clear to you. Besides, in this case, notice this: the crime was committed at eleven twenty in the evening, as the clock shows, and the nocturnal visit reported by the concierges only took place at three in the morning.

Justice often falls prey to these convictions that compel events to conform to the initial explanation provided. The unfortunate past of Victor Danègre, a repeat offender, drunkard, and debauchee, influenced the judge, and although no new circumstances emerged to support the two or three initial clues discovered, nothing could shake his resolve. He closed his investigation. A few weeks later, the hearings began.

They were embarrassed and languid. The president led them without enthusiasm. The public prosecutor attacked feebly. Under these conditions, Danègre's lawyer had an easy time. He pointed out the gaps and impossibilities in the prosecution's case. There was no material evidence. Who had forged the key, the essential key without which Danègre could not have locked the apartment door from the inside after he left? Who had seen that key, and what had become of it? Who had seen the murderer's knife, and what had become of it?

—And in any case, the lawyer concluded, prove that it was my client who killed. Prove that the author of the theft and the crime is not that mysterious figure who entered the house at three in the morning. The clock showed eleven o'clock, you say? So what? Can't one set the hands of a clock to whatever time suits them?

Victor Danègre was acquitted.

* * *

He left prison on a Friday at dusk, emaciated, depressed after six months in a cell. The investigation, the solitude, the debates, the jury's deliberations had filled him with a sickening dread. At night, terrible nightmares and visions of the scaffold haunted him. He trembled with fever and terror.

Under the name Anatole Dufour, he rented a small room in the heights of Montmartre and lived by taking on odd jobs, tinkering here and there.

A miserable life! Three times he was hired by three different employers, and each time he was recognized and promptly dismissed.

Often he noticed, or thought he noticed, that men were following him—men from the police, he had no doubt—who were determined to trap him in some way. And he could already feel the rough grip of the hand that would seize him by the collar.

One evening, while dining at a local caterer, someone sat down across from him. It was a man in his forties, dressed in a somewhat questionable black frock coat. He ordered soup, vegetables, and a liter of wine.

After he finished his soup, he turned his gaze toward Danègre and looked at him for a long time.

Danègre paled. This man was certainly one of those who had been following him for weeks. What did he want? Danègre tried to stand up. He couldn't. His legs wobbled beneath him.

The man poured himself a glass of wine and filled Danègre's glass.

— Shall we toast, comrade?

Victor stammered:

— Yes… yes… to your health, comrade.

— To your health, Victor Danègre.

The other man flinched:

— Me!… me!… but no… I swear…

— What do you swear? That you're not you? The countess's servant?

— What servant? My name is Dufour. Ask the boss.

— Dufour, Anatole, yes, for the boss, but Danègre for the law, Victor Danègre.

— Not true! Not true! You've been lied to.

The newcomer pulled a card from his pocket and handed it over. Victor read: "Grimaudan, former inspector of the Sûreté. Confidential information." He flinched.

— You're with the police?

— I'm no longer with them, but I enjoyed the work, and I continue in a more… lucrative manner. Occasionally, you come across cases of gold… like yours.

— Mine?

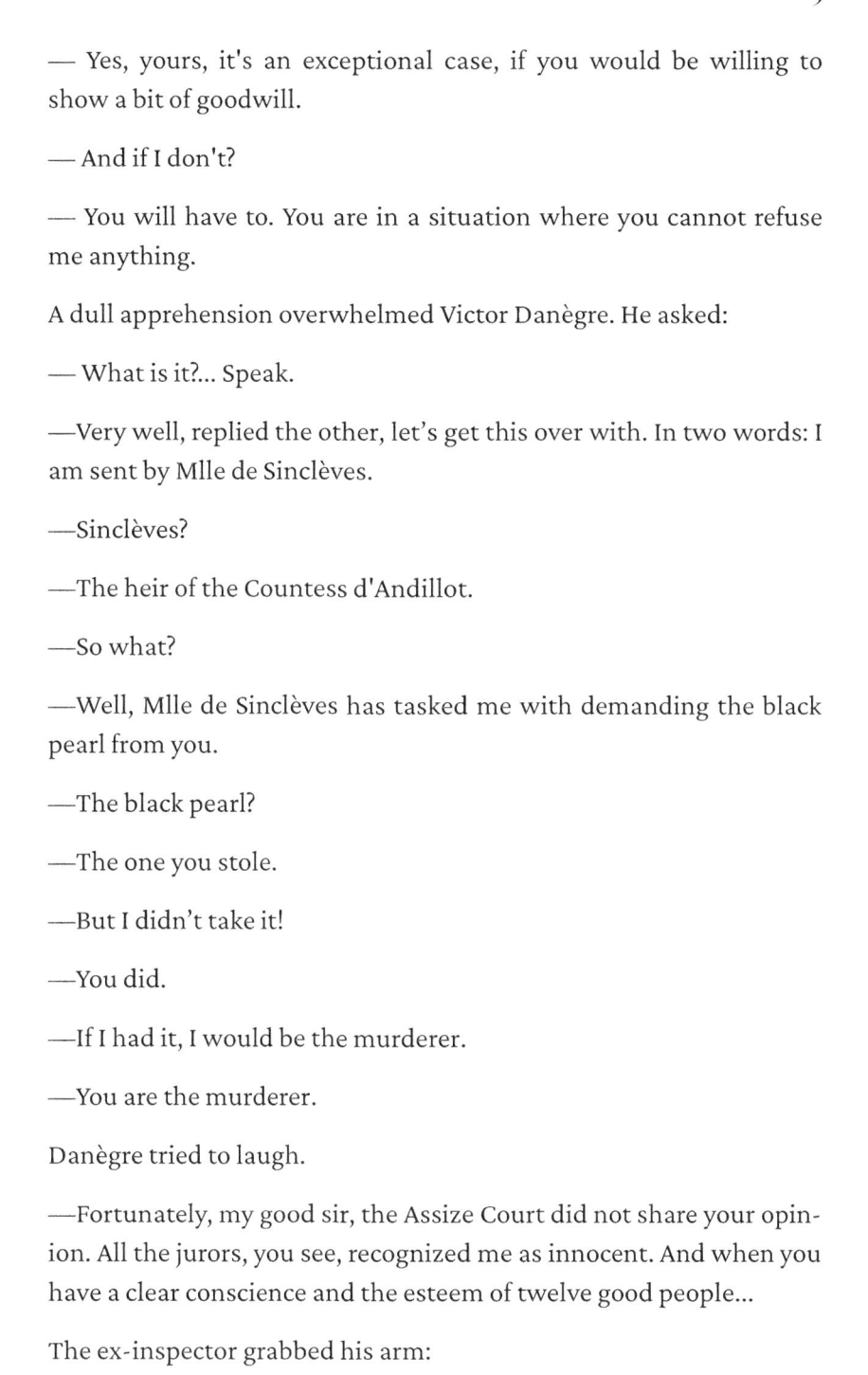

— Yes, yours, it's an exceptional case, if you would be willing to show a bit of goodwill.

— And if I don't?

— You will have to. You are in a situation where you cannot refuse me anything.

A dull apprehension overwhelmed Victor Danègre. He asked:

— What is it?... Speak.

—Very well, replied the other, let's get this over with. In two words: I am sent by Mlle de Sinclèves.

—Sinclèves?

—The heir of the Countess d'Andillot.

—So what?

—Well, Mlle de Sinclèves has tasked me with demanding the black pearl from you.

—The black pearl?

—The one you stole.

—But I didn't take it!

—You did.

—If I had it, I would be the murderer.

—You are the murderer.

Danègre tried to laugh.

—Fortunately, my good sir, the Assize Court did not share your opinion. All the jurors, you see, recognized me as innocent. And when you have a clear conscience and the esteem of twelve good people...

The ex-inspector grabbed his arm:

—No more phrases, my friend. Listen to me very carefully and weigh my words; they are worth it. Danègre, three weeks before the crime, you stole the key from the cook that opens the service door, and you had a similar key made by Outard, the locksmith, at 244 Oberkampf Street.

—Not true, not true, grumbled Victor, no one saw that key... it doesn't exist.

—Here it is.

After a silence, Grimaudan continued:

—You killed the Countess with a knife purchased at the bazaar on the Republic, the very day you ordered your key. The blade is triangular and has a groove.

—This is all nonsense, you're just talking randomly. No one saw the knife.

—Here it is.

Victor Danègre flinched. The ex-inspector went on:

—There are rust stains on it. Do I need to explain where they came from?

—And then?... you have a key and a knife... Who can prove they belonged to me?

—First the locksmith, and then the employee from whom you bought the knife. I've already jogged their memories. In front of you, they will certainly recognize you.

He spoke dryly and harshly, with a terrifying precision. Danègre was convulsed with fear. Neither the judge nor the president of the court nor the public prosecutor had pressed him so closely or seen so clearly into matters he himself no longer perceived distinctly.

Still, he tried once more to feign indifference.

—If that's all your evidence!

—I have this left. You left the scene of the crime by the same route. But, in the middle of the room with the robes, gripped by fear, you must have leaned against the wall to steady yourself.

—How do you know that? Victor stammered... no one could possibly know.

—Justice, no, none of those gentlemen from the prosecution would think to light a candle and examine the walls. But if they did, they would find a very faint red mark on the white plaster, clear enough to reveal the imprint of the front of your thumb, still damp with blood that you pressed against the wall. And you know that in anthropometry, this is one of the main means of identification.

Victor Danègre was pale. Drops of sweat rolled from his forehead onto the table. He looked at this strange man, who spoke of his crime as if he had been an invisible witness, with the eyes of a madman.

He lowered his head, defeated and powerless. For months he had fought against everyone. Against this man, he felt there was nothing he could do.

—If I return the pearl to you, he stammered, how much will you give me?

—Nothing.

—What! You're joking! I would give you something worth thousands and hundreds of thousands, and I would get nothing in return?

—Yes, your life.

The wretched man shuddered. Grimaudan added, in an almost gentle tone:

—Come now, Danègre, this pearl has no value for you. It's impossible for you to sell it. What's the point of keeping it?

—There are fences… and sooner or later, at any price…

—Sooner or later, it will be too late.

—Why?

—Why? Because justice will have caught up with you, and this time, with the evidence I will provide—the knife, the key, the thumbprint—you're finished, my friend.

Victor clutched his head with both hands and thought. He felt lost, indeed, irretrievably lost, and at the same time, an overwhelming fatigue washed over him, an immense need for rest and surrender.

He murmured:

—When do you need it?

—Tonight, before one o'clock.

—Otherwise?

—Otherwise, I will mail this letter in which Mlle de Sinclèves denounces you to the public prosecutor.

Danègre poured himself two glasses of wine, which he drank back to back, then, getting up:

—Pay the bill, and let's go… I've had enough of this cursed business.

Night had fallen. The two men descended Lepic Street and followed the outer boulevards heading toward the Étoile. They walked silently, Victor very tired and hunched over.

At Parc Monceau, he said:

—It's over by the house…

—Of course! You only left it, before your arrest, to go to the tobacco shop.

—Here we are, Danègre said in a dull voice.

They walked along the garden gate and crossed a street where the tobacco shop was on the corner. Danègre stopped a few steps further. His legs wobbled. He fell onto a bench.

—Well? asked his companion.

—It's there.

—It's there! What are you singing to me?

—Yes, there, in front of us.

—in front of us! Come on, Danègre, you shouldn't...

—I repeat, it's there.

—Where?

—Between two cobblestones.

—Which ones?

—Look for them.

—Which ones? Grimaudan repeated.

Victor didn't reply.

—Ah! Perfect, you want to make a fool of me, my friend.

—No... but... I'm going to die of misery.

—And so, you're hesitating? Come on, I'll be generous. How much do you need?

—Enough for my steerage ticket to America.

—Agreed.

—And a hundred for initial expenses.

—You'll get two. Speak.

—Count the cobblestones, to the right of the gutter. It's between the twelfth and thirteenth.

—in the stream?

—Yes, at the bottom of the sidewalk.

Grimaudan looked around. Trams passed by, people walked past. But really! Who would suspect?...

He opened his pocket knife and drove it between the twelfth and thirteenth cobblestones.

—And what if it's not there?

—If no one saw me bend down and push it in, it's still there.

Could it really be there! The black pearl thrown into the mud of a stream, waiting for the first passerby! The black pearl… a fortune!

—How deep?

—About ten centimeters.

He dug into the wet sand. The tip of his knife struck something. With his fingers, he widened the hole.

He saw the black pearl.

—Here, that's your two hundred francs. I'll send you your ticket to America.

The next day, L'Écho de France published this brief article, which was reproduced by newspapers around the world:

Since yesterday, the famous black pearl is in the hands of Arsène Lupin, who took it back from the murderer of Countess d'Andillot. Soon, facsimiles of this precious jewel will be displayed in London, Saint Petersburg, Calcutta, Buenos Aires, and New York.

Arsène Lupin is awaiting the offers his correspondents will make.

* * *

—And thus, crime is always punished, and virtue rewarded, concluded Arsène Lupin as he revealed the details of the case to me.

—And thus, under the name of Grimaudan, former inspector of the Sûreté, you were chosen by fate to deprive the criminal of the benefits of his crime.

—Precisely. And I admit that this is one of the adventures I am most proud of. The forty minutes I spent in the countess's apartment, after confirming her death, are among the most astonishing and profound of my life. In those forty minutes, caught in the most inextricable situation, I reconstructed the crime and, with the help of a few clues, became certain that the culprit could only be a servant of the countess. Finally, I understood that to obtain the pearl, the servant needed to be arrested—but I left the vest button behind—yet there should not be irrefutable evidence of his guilt against him—and I picked up the knife forgotten on the carpet, took the key left in the lock, locked the door securely, and erased the fingerprints on the plaster of the dressing room. In my view, that was one of those flashes…

—Of genius, I interjected.

—Genius, if you will, that would not have illuminated the mind of an ordinary person. To guess in an instant the two terms of the problem—an arrest and an acquittal—using the formidable apparatus of justice to disrupt my man, to dull his senses, in short, to put him in a state of mind such that once free, he would inevitably, fatally, fall into the somewhat crude trap that I was setting for him!…

—A little? You mean a lot, because he was in no danger.

—Oh! not the slightest, since any acquittal is a definitive matter.

—Poor fellow…

—Poor fellow... Victor Danègre! you don't realize he's a murderer? It would have been the height of immorality for the black pearl to remain with him. He lives, just think, Danègre lives!

—And the black pearl belongs to you.

He took it out from one of the secret pockets of his wallet, examined it, caressed it with his fingers and with his misty eyes, and he sighed:

—What foolhardy and vain nobleman will possess this treasure? To which American billionaire is destined this small piece of beauty and luxury that adorned the white shoulders of Léontine Zalti, Countess d'Andillot?...

CHAPTER TEN
HERLOCK SHOLMÈS ARRIVES TOO LATE

It's strange how much you resemble Arsène Lupin, Velmont!

—You know him?

—Oh! like everyone else, from his photographs, none of which is like the others, but each leaves the impression of an identical face... which is very much yours.

Horace Velmont appeared somewhat vexed.

—Isn't that right, my dear Devanne! And you're not the first to point this out to me, believe me.

—It's just as well, insisted Devanne, that if you hadn't been recommended to me by my cousin from Estevan, and if you weren't the well-known painter whose beautiful seascapes I admire, I wonder if I might not have alerted the police about your presence in Dieppe.

The jest was met with general laughter. In the grand dining room of the Thibermesnil castle, alongside Velmont, were the village priest, Abbé Gélis, and about a dozen officers from the regiments maneuvering in the area, who had accepted the invitation from banker Georges Devanne and his mother. One of them exclaimed:

—But hasn't Arsène Lupin been spotted on the coast, after his famous heist on the express train from Paris to Le Havre?

—Exactly, that was three months ago, and the following week I met our excellent Velmont at the casino, who has since kindly honored me with a few visits—an enjoyable preamble to a more serious visit he will pay me one of these days… or rather one of these nights!

They laughed again and moved into the old guardroom, a vast, very high room that occupies the entire lower part of the Guillaume tower, where Georges Devanne has gathered the incomparable riches accumulated over the centuries by the lords of Thibermesnil. Dressers and credenzas, chandeliers and sconces adorn the space. Magnificent tapestries hang on the stone walls. The embrasures of the four windows are deep, equipped with benches, and finish with pointed arches featuring stained glass framed in lead. Between the door and the left window stands a monumental Renaissance-style library, on the pediment of which is inscribed in gold letters, "Thibermesnil," and below, the proud motto of the family: "Fais ce que veulx."

And as they lit cigars, Devanne continued:

—Just hurry up, Velmont, it's your last night here.

—And why is that? replied the painter, who was clearly taking the matter lightly.

Devanne was about to respond when his mother signaled him. But the excitement of dinner and the desire to engage his guests overtook him.

—Oh well! he murmured, I can speak now. There's no risk of indiscretion anymore.

They gathered around him with keen curiosity, and he declared, with the satisfied air of someone announcing significant news:

—Tomorrow, at four o'clock in the afternoon, Herlock Sholmes, the great English detective for whom no mystery is unsolvable, Herlock Sholmes, the most extraordinary solver of enigmas ever seen, the prodigious figure that seems entirely forged by a novelist's imagination, Herlock Sholmes will be my guest.

There was an uproar. Herlock Sholmes in Thibermesnil? Was this serious? Arsène Lupin was indeed in the area?

—Arsène Lupin and his gang are not far away. Not to mention the case of Baron Cahorn, to whom we can attribute the burglaries in Montigny, Gruchet, and Crasville, if not to our national thief? Today, it's my turn.

—And you have been warned, just like Baron Cahorn?

—The same trick doesn't work twice.

—So?

—So?... Here it is.

He stood up and pointed out a small empty space between two large folios on one of the library shelves:

—There was a book here, a book from the 16th century titled *The Chronicle of Thibermesnil*, which was the history of the castle since its construction by Duke Rollon on the site of a feudal fortress. It contained three engraved plates. One depicted an aerial view of the estate as a whole, the second showed the layout of the buildings, and the third—I draw your attention to this—illustrated the path of a hidden passage, one of whose exits opens outside the first line of the ramparts, while the other leads here, yes, to the very room we are in. Now, this book has been missing since last month.

—Goodness, said Velmont, that's a bad sign. But that alone isn't enough to warrant the intervention of Herlock Sholmes.

—Certainly, it would not have been enough if another fact had not occurred that gives full significance to what I have just told you. There was a second copy of this Chronicle at the National Library, and these two copies differed in certain details regarding the underground passage, such as the establishment of a profile and a scale, along with various annotations, not printed but written in ink and more or less faded. I was aware of these particulars, and I knew that the final layout could only be reconstructed through a meticulous comparison of the two maps. Now, the day after my copy disappeared, the one from the National Library was requested by a reader who took it away without it being possible to determine the circumstances under which the theft occurred.

Exclamations greeted these words.

—This time, the matter is getting serious.

—Indeed, this time, said Devanne, the police were stirred into action, and there was a double investigation, which, however, yielded no results.

—Like all those involving Arsène Lupin.

—Precisely. It was then that it occurred to me to ask for the assistance of Herlock Sholmes, who replied that he was very eager to make contact with Arsène Lupin.

—What glory for Arsène Lupin! said Velmont! But if our national thief, as you call him, has no plans regarding Thibermesnil, will Herlock Sholmes just be twiddling his thumbs?

—There is something else that will interest him greatly: the discovery of the underground passage.

—What do you mean? You told us that one of the entrances opened to the countryside, the other in this very salon!

—Where? In which part of this room? The line that represents the underground passage on the maps ends on one side at a small circle marked with the two capital letters "T. G.", which probably stands for Tour Guillaume. But the tower is round, and who could determine at what point on the circle the drawing begins?

Devanne lit a second cigar and poured himself a glass of Benedictine. He was being pressed with questions. He smiled, pleased with the interest he had stirred. Finally, he said:

—The secret is lost. No one in the world knows it. According to legend, it was passed down from father to son among the powerful lords at their deathbeds, until the day when Geoffroy, the last of his name, had his head chopped off on the scaffold, on the 7th of Thermidor, Year II, at the age of nineteen.

—But, for a century now, there must have been searches?

—There have been searches, but in vain. When I bought the castle from the great-grandnephew of the revolutionary Leribourg, I had excavations done myself. What was the point? Consider that this tower, surrounded by water, is connected to the castle at only one point, which means the underground passage must run beneath the old ditches. The plan from the National Library shows a series of four staircases with forty-eight steps, suggesting a depth of more than ten meters. And the scale attached to the other plan indicates the distance to be two hundred meters. In reality, the whole issue lies here, between this floor, this ceiling, and these walls. Honestly, I must admit I hesitate to tear them down.

—And there are no clues?

—None.

Abbé Gélis interjected:

—Mr. Devanne, we must take into account two citations.

"Oh!" exclaimed Devanne, laughing, "The priest is an archive digger, a great reader of memoirs, and everything related to Thibermesnil fascinates him. But the explanation he's talking about only serves to confuse things."

"But what else?"

"Do you really care?"

"Very much."

"Then you'll know that from his readings, it turns out that two kings of France have the key to the riddle."

"Two kings of France!"

"Henry IV and Louis XVI."

"Those are not just any kings. And how does the abbot know this?"

"Oh! It's quite simple," Devanne continued. "The day before the Battle of Arques, King Henry IV came to dinner and stayed overnight at this castle. At eleven o'clock in the evening, Louise de Tancarville, the most beautiful lady in Normandy, was introduced to him through a secret passage with the help of Duke Edgard, who, on this occasion, revealed a family secret. This secret, Henry IV later entrusted to his minister Sully, who recounts the anecdote in his 'Royal State Economies' without offering any further commentary other than this incomprehensible phrase:

'The axe whirls in the trembling air, but the wing opens, and one goes to God.'

There was a silence, and Velmont chuckled:

"That's not exactly crystal clear."

"Isn't it? The priest believes that Sully noted the key to the riddle there, without betraying the secret of the scribes to whom he dictated his memoirs."

"The hypothesis is clever."

"I agree, but what is this axe that spins, and this bird that flies away?"

"And what goes to God?"

"A mystery!"

Velmont resumed:

"And did good Louis XVI also have a lady to visit when he had the secret passage opened?"

—I don't know. All that can be said is that Louis XVI stayed in Thibermesnil in 1784, and that the famous iron cabinet found in the Louvre, based on Gamain's denunciation, contained a paper with these words written by him: "Thibermesnil: 2-6-12."

Horace Velmont burst out laughing:

—Victory! The darkness is clearing more and more. Two times six makes twelve.

—Laugh as you wish, sir, said the abbé, it doesn't change the fact that these two quotes hold the solution, and someday someone will come who knows how to interpret them.

—Herlock Sholmes first, said Devanne... Unless Arsène Lupin gets there first. What do you think, Velmont?

Velmont stood up, placed his hand on Devanne's shoulder, and declared:

—I believe that based on the information provided by your book and that of the Library, there was a piece of crucial information missing, which you kindly offered me. Thank you for that.

—So what?...

—So now, with the axe having swung, the bird having flown, and two times six making twelve, I just need to get started.

—Without wasting a minute.

—Without wasting a second! Do I not need to break into your castle tonight, that is, before Herlock Sholmes arrives?

—It is true that you have just enough time. Would you like me to take you?

—To Dieppe?

—To Dieppe. I will take the opportunity to bring back Mr. and Mme d'Androl and a young lady who is a friend of theirs arriving on the midnight train.

And addressing the officers, Devanne added:

—Besides, we will all meet here for lunch tomorrow, right, gentlemen? I am counting on you, since this castle is to be besieged by your regiments and stormed at eleven o'clock.

The invitation was accepted, they parted ways, and a moment later, a 20-30 Golden Star took Devanne and Velmont on the road to Dieppe. Devanne dropped the painter off in front of the casino and headed to the train station.

At midnight, his friends were getting off the train. At half past midnight, the car passed through the gates of Thibermesnil. At one o'clock, after a light supper served in the lounge, everyone retired. Gradually, all the lights went out. The great silence of the night enveloped the castle.

* * *

But the moon pushed away the clouds that had obscured it, and through two of the windows, filled the lounge with white light. This lasted only a moment. Very quickly, the moon hid behind the curtain of the hills. And then came the darkness. The silence deepened with the thicker shadow. Occasionally, the creaking of furniture disturbed it, or the rustling of reeds by the pond that washes against the old walls with its green waters.

The clock ticked off the endless string of seconds. It struck two o'clock. Then, once again, the seconds fell hastily and monotonously into the heavy peace of the night. Then three o'clock chimed.

And suddenly something snapped, like the disc of a signal that opens and closes when a train passes. A fine beam of light shot across the living room from one side to the other, like an arrow leaving behind a sparkling trail. It emanated from the central groove of a pilaster where, on the right, the pediment of the library rested. It first settled on the opposite panel in a bright circle, then moved around as if searching the shadows with an anxious gaze, before vanishing only to burst forth again, while a part of the library spun around, revealing a large arch-shaped opening.

A man entered, holding an electric lantern. Two others appeared, carrying a roll of ropes and various tools. The first man inspected the room, listened, and said:

—Call the comrades.

From the underground came eight sturdy comrades with energetic faces. And the move began.

It was quick. Arsène Lupin moved from one piece of furniture to another, examined them, and based on their dimensions or artistic value, either spared them or ordered:

—Take it away!

And the item was removed, swallowed by the gaping mouth of the tunnel, dispatched into the depths of the earth.

Thus, six Louis XV armchairs and six chairs, Aubusson tapestries, Gouthière-signed girandoles, two Fragonards, a Nattier, a bust by Houdon, and various statuettes were swiftly whisked away. Sometimes Lupin lingered before a magnificent sideboard or a stunning painting and sighed:

—Too heavy, that one... too big... what a shame!

And he continued his appraisal.

In forty minutes, the living room was "cleared out," as Arsène put it. And all of this was done in admirable order, without a sound, as if all the objects handled by these men were padded with thick cotton.

He then said to the last of them, who was leaving with a cart signed Boulle:

— There's no need to come back. It's understood, right? As soon as the truck is loaded, you head straight to the Roquefort barn.

— But what about you, boss?

— Just leave me the motorcycle.

Once the man was gone, he pushed the movable panel of the bookcase back into place, and after erasing all traces of the move and the footprints left behind, he lifted a door and stepped into a corridor that connected the tower to the castle. In the middle stood a display case, and it was because of this display case that Arsène Lupin had pursued his investigations.

It contained wonders, a unique collection of watches, snuff boxes, rings, chatelaines, and miniatures of exquisite craftsmanship. With a pair of pliers, he forced the lock, and it gave him indescribable pleasure to seize these jewels of gold and silver, these small works of such precious and delicate art.

He had a large canvas bag slung over his shoulder, specially designed for these finds. He filled it up. He also stuffed the pockets of his jacket, pants, and waistcoat. And he was closing his left arm around a pile of those beaded reticules so cherished by our ancestors, and which the current fashion seeks so passionately... when a faint noise caught his ear.

He listened: he was not mistaken; the noise was becoming clearer.

And suddenly he remembered: at the end of the hallway, an interior staircase led to an apartment that had been unoccupied until now, but which was reserved for the young girl that Devanne had gone to fetch in Dieppe, along with his friends from Androl.

With a quick motion, he pressed the button of his lantern: it went out. He had barely reached the window frame when the door at the top of the staircase opened, and a faint light illuminated the hallway.

He had the sensation—since he was half-hidden by a curtain, he could not see—that someone was carefully descending the first steps. He hoped she wouldn't come any further. However, she did come down and advanced several steps into the room. But then she let out a cry. She must have caught sight of the broken display case, which was three-quarters empty.

From the scent, he recognized the presence of a woman. Her clothing brushed against the curtain that concealed him, and he felt as if he could hear her heartbeat, and that she too sensed the presence of another being behind her, in the shadows, within reach of her hand... He thought to himself, "She is scared... she is going to leave... it's impossible for her not to leave." But she did not leave. The candle that trembled in her hand steadied. She turned around, hesitated for a moment, seemed to listen to the frightening silence, then suddenly pulled aside the curtain.

They saw each other.

Arsène murmured, shaken:

—You... you... Miss.

It was Miss Nelly.

Miss Nelly! The passenger of the transatlantic ship, the one who had intertwined her dreams with those of the young man during that unforgettable crossing, the one who had witnessed his arrest, and who, rather than betray him, had made the lovely gesture of throwing into the sea the Kodak where he had hidden the jewels and the banknotes... Miss Nelly! The dear and smiling creature whose image had so often saddened or delighted his long hours in prison!

The chance that brought them face to face in this castle at this hour of the night was so incredible that they remained still and silent, astonished, as if hypnotized by the fantastic appearance they presented to each other.

Tottering, overwhelmed with emotion, Miss Nelly had to sit down.

He stood before her. And gradually, over the interminable seconds that passed, he became aware of the impression he must be giving at that moment, his arms laden with trinkets, his pockets stuffed, and his bag overflowing. A great confusion washed over him, and he blushed at finding himself there, in this ugly position of a thief caught red-handed. For her, from now on, no matter what happened, he was the thief, the one who puts his hand in others' pockets, the one who picks locks and sneaks in silently.

One of the watches rolled onto the carpet, another followed. And more things were about to slip from his arms, which he didn't know how to hold onto. Then, suddenly deciding, he dropped part of the items onto the chair, emptied his pockets, and freed himself of his bag.

He felt more at ease in front of Nelly and took a step towards her, intending to speak. But she recoiled, then quickly stood up, as if struck by fear, and rushed into the living room. The curtain closed behind her, and he followed. She was there, stunned, trembling, her eyes filled with terror as they surveyed the vast, devastated room.

He immediately said to her:

— At three o'clock tomorrow, everything will be back in place... The furniture will be brought back...

She did not respond, and he repeated:

— Tomorrow, at three o'clock, I promise... Nothing in the world will stop me from keeping my promise... Tomorrow, at three o'clock...

A long silence hung over them. He did not dare break it, and the girl's distress caused him real pain. Gently, without a word, he stepped away from her.

And he thought:

— Let her go!... Let her feel free to leave!... Let her not be afraid of me!...

But suddenly she flinched and stammered:

— Listen... footsteps... I hear someone walking...

He looked at her in surprise. She seemed shaken, as if sensing danger approaching.

— I don't hear anything, he said, and even if I did...

— What! We must flee... quickly, run away...

— Flee... why?

— It is necessary... it is necessary... Oh! don't stay...

In a flash, she ran to the entrance of the gallery and listened intently. No, there was no one. Perhaps the noise was coming from outside?... She waited a second, then, reassured, turned back.

Arsène Lupin had vanished.

* * *

At the very moment Devanne discovered the looting of his castle, he thought to himself: it's Velmont who did this, and Velmont is none other than Arsène Lupin. Everything made sense this way, and nothing made sense any other way. This idea barely crossed his mind, as it seemed so implausible that Velmont could be anything but Velmont, the well-known painter, the circle companion of his cousin d'Estevan. And when the gendarmerie brigadier, promptly alerted, arrived, Devanne didn't even think to share this absurd suspicion with him.

All morning at Thibermesnil, there was an indescribable hustle and bustle. The gendarmes, the rural guard, the police commissioner from Dieppe, the villagers—everyone was bustling in the corridors, in the park, or around the castle. The approach of the troops on maneuvers, the crack of gunfire, added to the picturesque nature of the scene.

The initial searches yielded no clues. Since the windows had not been broken nor the doors forced, there was no doubt that the move had been carried out through the secret exit. Yet, on the carpet, there were no footprints, and on the walls, no unusual marks.

One unexpected thing did stand out, clearly showing Arsène Lupin's flair: the famous Chronicle of the 16th century had returned to its former place, and beside it was a similar book, which was none other than the stolen copy from the National Library.

At eleven o'clock, the officers arrived. Devanne greeted them cheerfully—despite the annoyance caused by the loss of such artistic treasures, his fortune allowed him to endure it without ill humor. His friends Androl and Nelly came downstairs.

Once the introductions were made, it became apparent that one guest was missing: Horace Velmont. Would he not be coming?

His absence would have raised suspicions in Georges Devanne. But precisely at noon, he entered. Devanne exclaimed:

—At last! Here you are!

—Am I not punctual?

—You are, but you could have easily been late... after such a restless night! Because you know the news?

—What news?

—You've robbed the castle.

—Come now!

—As I tell you. But first, offer your arm to Miss Underdown, and let's sit down... Miss, may I...

He stopped, struck by the young girl's agitation. Then, suddenly recalling:

—That's right, speaking of which, you traveled with Arsène Lupin once... before his arrest... The resemblance surprises you, doesn't it?

She did not respond. In front of her, Velmont smiled. He bowed, and she took his arm. He led her to her seat and sat down across from her.

During lunch, the only topic of conversation was Arsène Lupin, the stolen furniture, the underground passages, and Herlock Sholmes. Only at the end of the meal, as other subjects were introduced, did Velmont join the conversation. He was alternately amusing and serious, eloquent and witty. And everything he said seemed directed solely at engaging the young girl. Deep in thought, she appeared not to hear him.

The coffee was served on the terrace overlooking the courtyard and the formal French garden beside the main façade. In the middle of the lawn, the regimental band began to play, and the crowd of peasants and soldiers spread out through the park.

Meanwhile, Nelly recalled Arsène Lupin's promise: "Everything will be there by three o'clock, I assure you."

At three o'clock! The hands of the large clock adorning the right wing showed two forty. She found herself glancing at it constantly. She was also watching Velmont, who was comfortably rocking in an easy chair.

Two fifty... two fifty-five... a sort of impatience, mixed with anxiety, gripped the young girl. Was it possible that the miracle would happen, and that it would happen exactly on time, while the castle, the courtyard, and the countryside were filled with people, and at that very moment the public prosecutor and the investigating judge were pursuing their inquiry?

And yet... yet, Arsène Lupin had promised with such solemnity! It will be as he said, she thought, impressed by all the energy, authority, and certainty that man exuded. And it no longer seemed like a miracle to her, but a natural event that was bound to happen by the force of circumstances.

For a moment, their eyes met. She blushed and turned her head away.

Three o'clock... The first stroke rang out, the second, the third... Horace Velmont took out his watch, looked up at the clock, then put his watch back in his pocket. A few seconds passed. Then the crowd parted around the lawn, making way for two carriages that had just passed through the gate of the park, each drawn by two horses. They were those supply wagons that follow regiments, carrying the officers' rations and the soldiers' gear. They stopped in front of the porch. A sergeant jumped from one of the seats and asked for Mr. Devanne.

Devanne rushed down the steps. Under the tarps, he saw his furniture, paintings, and artworks, all carefully arranged and well-wrapped.

When asked questions, the quartermaster responded by showing the order he had received from the duty sergeant, which the sergeant had taken from the morning report. By this order, the second company of the fourth battalion was to ensure that the furniture stored at the Halleux crossroads, in the Arques forest, was delivered at three o'clock to Mr. Georges Devanne, owner of the Thibermesnil castle. Signed: Colonel Beauvel.

"At the crossroads," the sergeant added, "everything was ready, lined up on the grass, and under the watch of... passersby. I thought it was funny, but still! The order was categorical."

One of the officers examined the signature: it was perfectly forged but false.

The music had stopped playing, the wagons were unloaded, and the furniture was brought back inside.

Amidst this commotion, Nelly remained alone at the end of the terrace. She was serious and anxious, troubled by confused thoughts she did not try to articulate. Suddenly, she spotted Velmont approaching. She wished to avoid him, but the angle of the balustrade that bordered the terrace surrounded her on two sides, and a line of large boxes containing shrubs, orange trees, oleanders, and bamboo left her no escape other than the path along which the young man was advancing. She did not move. A ray of sunlight flickered on her golden hair, stirred by the delicate leaves of a bamboo. Someone whispered very softly:

"I kept my promise from last night."

Arsène Lupin was beside her, and there was no one else around them.

He repeated, hesitantly, in a timid voice:

"I kept my promise from last night."

He was waiting for a word of thanks, at least a gesture that would show the interest she took in this act. She remained silent.

This disdain irritated Arsène Lupin, and at the same time, he felt deeply everything that separated him from Nelly now that she knew the truth. He wished to exonerate himself, to find excuses, to show her his life in all its boldness and greatness. But even before he spoke, the words felt harsh to him, and he sensed the absurdity and insolence of any explanation. So he murmured sadly, overwhelmed by a flood of memories:

—How far away the past seems! Do you remember the long hours on the bridge in Provence? Ah! You had, just like today, a rose in your hand, a pale rose like this one... I asked you for it... you didn't seem to hear... Yet, after you left, I found the rose... undoubtedly forgotten... I kept it...

She still did not respond. She seemed very far from him. He continued:

—In memory of those hours, do not think of what you know. Let the past connect to the present! Let me not be the one you saw last night, but the one from before, and let your eyes look at me, even if just for a second, as they used to... Please... Am I no longer the same?

She lifted her eyes, as he had asked, and looked at him. Then, without a word, she placed her finger on a ring he wore on his index finger. Only the band was visible, but the setting, turned inward, was made of a marvelous ruby.

Arsène Lupin blushed. That ring belonged to Georges Devanne.

He smiled bitterly:

—You are right. What has been will always be. Arsène Lupin is and can only be Arsène Lupin, and between you and him, there cannot even be a memory... Forgive me... I should have understood that my mere presence beside you is an affront...

He stepped back along the railing, holding his hat in hand. Nelly walked past him. He was tempted to stop her, to plead with her. He lacked the courage, and he followed her with his eyes, just as he had on that distant day when she crossed the gangway on the New York dock. She climbed the steps leading to the door. For a moment, her delicate silhouette was outlined among the marbles of the vestibule. He no longer saw her.

A cloud obscured the sun. Arsène Lupin stood still, observing the trace of small footsteps imprinted in the sand. Suddenly, he shuddered: on the bamboo crate against which Nelly had leaned lay the rose, the pale rose he had not dared to ask for... Forgotten, no doubt, just like her? But was it forgotten intentionally or out of distraction?

He seized it eagerly. Petals came loose from it. He picked them up one by one like relics...

—Come now, he told himself, I have nothing more to do here. Let's think about retreating. Especially since if Herlock Sholmes gets involved, it could turn bad.

* * *

The park was deserted. However, near the pavilion that overlooks the entrance, there stood a group of gendarmes. He plunged into the thickets, climbed over the enclosing wall, and took a path winding through the fields to reach the nearest train station. He had not walked for ten minutes when the path narrowed, enclosed between two embankments, and as he entered this narrow passage, someone was coming toward him from the opposite direction.

He was a man of about fifty, quite stout, with a clean-shaven face, and his suit suggested a foreign appearance. He carried a heavy cane in one hand, and a satchel hung from his neck.

They crossed paths. The stranger said, with a barely perceptible English accent:

—Excuse me, sir… is this the road to the castle?

—Straight ahead, sir, and to the left as soon as you reach the foot of the wall. We are eagerly awaiting you.

—Oh!

—Yes, my friend Devanne informed us of your visit as early as last night.

—Too bad for Mr. Devanne if he spoke too much.

—And I am glad to be the first to greet you. Herlock Sholmes has no more fervent admirer than I.

There was a barely noticeable hint of irony in his voice that he immediately regretted, for Herlock Sholmes looked him up and down, with a gaze that was both enveloping and piercing, making Arsène Lupin feel as if he were captured, imprisoned, and recorded by that look more accurately and fundamentally than he had ever been by any photographic device.

—The snapshot is taken, he thought. No need to disguise myself around this fellow. Only… has he recognized me?

They exchanged greetings. But then a sound of footsteps echoed, the sound of horses galloping accompanied by the clinking of steel. It was the gendarmes. The two men had to press themselves against the bank, in the tall grass, to avoid being jostled. The gendarmes passed, and since they were following each other at some distance, it took quite a while. And Lupin thought:

—Everything depends on this question: has he recognized me? If so, there's a good chance he will take advantage of the situation. The problem is nerve-wracking.

When the last horseman passed them, Herlock Sholmes stood up and, without saying a word, brushed the dust off his clothes. The strap of his bag was caught on a thorny branch. Arsène Lupin rushed to help. For a brief moment, they assessed each other. And if anyone had been able to witness that instant, it would have been an emotional sight—the first meeting of these two strange men, both powerfully armed, truly superior in their own ways, destined by their unique skills to collide like two equal forces pushed together by the order of things across space.

Then the Englishman said:

"Thank you, sir."

"At your service," Lupin replied.

They parted ways. Lupin headed toward the station while Herlock Sholmes made his way to the castle.

The examining magistrate and the prosecutor had left after fruitless searches, and everyone awaited Herlock Sholmes with a curiosity justified by his great reputation. There was some disappointment at his appearance as an ordinary bourgeois, which was so different from the image people had of him. He was nothing like the heroic figure, the enigmatic and diabolical character conjured by the name Herlock Sholmes. However, Devanne exclaimed with exuberance:

"Finally, Master, it's you! What a joy! I've been hoping for this for so long… I'm almost glad for everything that has happened, since it gives me the pleasure of seeing you. But by the way, how did you arrive?"

"By train!"

"What a pity! I had sent my car to the station for you."

"An official arrival, right? With drums and music! An excellent way to make my job easier," grumbled the Englishman.

This unwelcoming tone puzzled Devanne, who, trying to lighten the mood, replied:

—The task, fortunately, is easier than I had written to you.

—And why is that?

—Because the theft took place last night.

—If you hadn't announced my visit, sir, it's likely that the theft wouldn't have happened last night.

—And when would it have occurred?

—Tomorrow, or another day.

—And in that case?

—Lupin would have been caught in a trap.

—And my furniture?

—Would not have been taken.

—My furniture is here.

—Here?

—It was brought back at three o'clock.

—By Lupin?

—By two military trucks.

Herlock Sholmes violently pushed his hat down on his head and adjusted his bag; but Devanne, in a flurry, exclaimed:

—What are you doing?

—I'm leaving.

—And why is that?

—Your furniture is here, Arsène Lupin is far away. My role is finished.

—But I absolutely need your help, dear sir. What happened yesterday could happen again tomorrow, since we don't know the most important thing: how Arsène Lupin entered, how he left, and why, a few hours later, he returned the items.

—Ah! you don't know…

The idea of a secret to uncover softened Herlock Sholmes.

—Very well, let's investigate. But quickly, shall we? And as much as possible, alone.

The phrase clearly indicated the assistants. Devanne understood and led the Englishman into the parlor. In a curt tone, with phrases that seemed rehearsed, and oh so sparingly! Sholmes asked him questions about the previous evening, about the guests who were present, about the regulars of the castle. Then he examined the two volumes of the Chronicle, compared the maps of the underground passages, had the quotes noted by Abbé Gélis repeated to him, and asked:

—It was yesterday that you first mentioned these two quotes?

—Yes, yesterday.

—You had never shared them with Mr. Horace Velmont?

—Never.

—Alright. Order your car. I'll be leaving in an hour.

—In an hour!

—Arsène Lupin took no longer to solve the problem you posed him.

—Me!... I posed it to him...

—Ah! yes, Arsène Lupin and Velmont are the same person.

—I suspected as much... oh, that scoundrel!

—Now, last night at ten o'clock, you provided Lupin with the missing pieces of truth he had been searching for weeks. And during the night, Lupin found the time to understand, gather his gang, and rob you. I have the ambition to be just as quick.

He walked back and forth across the room, deep in thought, then sat down, crossed his long legs, and closed his eyes.

Devanne waited, feeling quite uneasy.

—Is he sleeping? Is he thinking?

Just in case, he stepped out to give some orders. When he returned, he saw him at the bottom of the gallery staircase, on his knees, examining the carpet.

—What's going on?

—Look... there... those wax stains...

—Indeed... and they're quite fresh...

—And you can also see them at the top of the staircase, and even more around that display case that Arsène Lupin broke into, and from which he took the trinkets to place them on this chair.

—And what do you conclude from this?

—Nothing. All these facts would undoubtedly explain the restitution he carried out. But that's a side of the issue I don't have time to address. The main thing is the layout of the underground passage.

—You still hope...

—I don't hope, I know. There is, isn't there, a chapel two or three hundred meters from the castle?

—A ruined chapel, where the tomb of Duke Rollon is located.

—Tell your driver to wait for us near that chapel.

—My driver hasn't returned yet... I should be informed... But, from what I see, you believe the underground passage leads to the chapel. What evidence do you have...

Herlock Sholmes interrupted him:

—I would ask you, sir, to provide me with a ladder and a lantern.

—Ah! You need a lantern and a ladder?

—Apparently, since I am requesting them.

Devanne, somewhat taken aback by this blunt logic, rang a bell. The two items were brought to him.

Orders then followed with the rigor and precision of military commands.

—Place this ladder against the library, to the left of the word Thibermesnil...

Devanne set up the ladder, and the Englishman continued:

—Further to the left... to the right... Halt!... Climb... Good... All the letters of this word are raised, correct?

—Yes.

—Let's focus on the letter H. Does it turn in one direction or the other?

Devanne grasped the letter H and exclaimed:

—Yes, it turns! to the right, and a quarter of a circle! Who told you this?...

Without responding, Herlock Sholmes continued:

—Can you, from where you are, reach the letter R? Yes... Move it several times, as you would a latch that you push and pull.

Devanne moved the letter R. To his great astonishment, an internal mechanism was triggered.

—Perfect, said Herlock Sholmes. Now you just need to slide your ladder to the other end, that is, to the end of the word Thibermesnil... Good... And now, if I'm not mistaken, if everything unfolds as it should, the letter L will open like a hatch.

With a certain solemnity, Devanne grasped the letter L. The letter L opened, but Devanne tumbled down from his ladder, as the entire section of the library located between the first and last letter of the word pivoted on itself, revealing the entrance to the underground passage.

Herlock Sholmès said, in a phlegmatic tone:

—Are you hurt?

—No, no, Devanne replied as he got back up, not hurt, but bewildered, I admit... those letters moving... that gaping underground passage...

—And then? Isn't that exactly in accordance with Sully's quote?

—In what way, sir?

—Well! The H twirls, the R trembles, and the L opens... and that is what allowed Henry IV to receive Mlle de Tancarville at an unusual hour.

—But Louis XVI? Devanne asked, astonished.

—Louis XVI was a great blacksmith and skilled locksmith. I read a "Treatise on Combination Locks" attributed to him. It was only fitting for Thibermesnil to present this mechanical masterpiece to his master. For the record, the king wrote: 2-6-12, meaning H. R. L., the second, sixth, and twelfth letters of the word.

—Ah! Perfect, I'm starting to understand... But here's the thing... While I can figure out how to exit this room, I can't explain how Lupin managed to enter it. Because, mark my words, he came from outside.

Herlock Sholmès lit the lantern and stepped a few paces into the underground passage.

—Look, the entire mechanism is visible here, like the springs of a clock, and all the letters are found upside down. Lupin only had to manipulate them from this side of the partition.

—What proof?

—What proof? Look at that puddle of oil. Lupin even anticipated that the gears would need to be lubricated, Herlock Sholmès said, not without admiration.

—So he knew about the other exit?

—Just as I do. Follow me.

—Into the tunnel?

—Are you afraid?

—No, but are you sure you can find your way?

—With my eyes closed.

They first descended twelve steps, then another twelve, and then two more sets of twelve. After that, they entered a long corridor with brick walls showing signs of successive restorations and damp in places. The floor was wet.

—We're going under the pond, Devanne noted, feeling far from reassured.

The corridor led to a staircase with twelve steps, followed by three more sets of twelve steps that they climbed with difficulty, finally emerging into a small chamber carved from the rock. The path didn't go any further.

—Good heavens, murmured Herlock Sholmes, just bare walls, this is becoming awkward.

—Should we turn back? Devanne suggested quietly, because, really, I don't see any need to know more. I'm already enlightened.

But, having looked up, the Englishman let out a sigh of relief: above them was the same mechanism as at the entrance. He only had to manipulate the three letters. A block of granite shifted. On the other side was the tombstone of Duke Rollon, engraved with the twelve letters in relief: "Thibermesnil." And they found themselves in the small ruined chapel that the Englishman had indicated.

—"And one goes all the way to God," meaning to the chapel, he said, recalling the end of the quote.

—Is it possible, Devanne exclaimed, bewildered by Herlock Sholmes's insight and quickness, is it possible that this simple indication was enough for you?

"Bah!" said the Englishman, "it was even useless. In the copy at the National Library, the line ends on the left, as you know, with a circle, and on the right, as you don't know, with a small cross, but so faint that it can only be seen with a magnifying glass. This cross obviously signifies the chapel where we are."

Poor Devanne couldn't believe his ears.

"It's unbelievable, miraculous, yet so childishly simple! How has no one ever solved this mystery?"

"Because no one has ever gathered the three or four necessary elements, that is, the two books and the citations... No one, except Arsène Lupin and me."

"But I also," Devanne objected, "and Abbé Gélis... We both knew as much as you did, and yet..."

Sholmès smiled.

"Mr. Devanne, not everyone is capable of deciphering riddles."

"But I've been searching for ten years. And you, in ten minutes..."

"Bah! It's just practice..."

They left the chapel, and the Englishman exclaimed:

"Look, a car is waiting!"

"But that's mine!"

"Yours? I thought the driver hadn't returned."

"Indeed... and I wonder..."

They approached the car, and Devanne called to the driver:

"Édouard, who told you to come here?"

"But, sir," replied the man, "it was Mr. Velmont."

"Mr. Velmont? So, you met him?"

"Near the station, and he told me to go to the chapel."

"To go to the chapel! But why?"

"To wait for sir... and sir's friend."

Devanne and Herlock Sholmès exchanged glances. Devanne said:

"He understood that the riddle would be child's play for you. That's a thoughtful gesture."

A satisfied smile creased the thin lips of the detective. He appreciated the gesture. He nodded and said:

—It's a man. Just by looking at him, I had already judged him.

—So you saw him?

—We crossed paths a little while ago.

—And you knew it was Horace Velmont, I mean Arsène Lupin?

—No, but I quickly guessed it… from a certain irony on his part.

—And you let him get away?

—Indeed, yes… I had a good opportunity… five gendarmes passed by.

—But, good heavens! that was the perfect chance to take advantage…

—Exactly, sir, the Englishman replied with hauteur, when it comes to an opponent like Arsène Lupin, Herlock Sholmes does not take advantage of opportunities… he creates them…

But time was pressing, and since Lupin had kindly sent the automobile, they had to take advantage of it without delay. Devanne and Herlock Sholmes settled into the back of the comfortable limousine. Édouard cranked the engine and they set off. Fields and clumps of trees passed by. The gentle undulations of the Pays de Caux flattened before them. Suddenly, Devanne's eyes were drawn to a small package placed in one of the pockets.

—Look, what's this? A package! And for whom? It's for you.

—For me?

—Read: "Mr. Herlock Sholmes, from Arsène Lupin."

The Englishman grabbed the package, untied it, and removed the two sheets of paper that wrapped it. It was a watch.

—Oh! he said, accompanying this exclamation with a gesture of anger...

—A watch, Devanne remarked, could it be...?

The Englishman did not respond.

—Look! It's your watch! Arsène Lupin is returning your watch to you! But if he's returning it, that means he took it... He took your watch! Ah! That's rich, the watch of Herlock Sholmes stolen by Arsène Lupin! God, that's funny! No, really... you'll have to forgive me... but I can't help it.

He laughed heartily, unable to contain himself. And when he had laughed enough, he declared, in a convinced tone:

—Oh! He is indeed a man.

The Englishman did not react. Until Dieppe, he did not say a word, his eyes fixed on the vanishing horizon. His silence was terrible, unfathomable, more intense than the fiercest rage. At the dock, he simply said, this time without anger, but with a tone that conveyed all the will and energy of the man:

—Yes, he is a man, and a man upon whose shoulder I will gladly place this hand that I extend to you, Mr. Devanne. And I have a feeling, you see, that Arsène Lupin and Herlock Sholmes will meet again one day... Yes, the world is too small for them not to cross paths... and when that day comes...

THE END

Printed in Great Britain
by Amazon